To Catherine

God Bless you

Robert D Bird

LOVE IS THE ANSWER

By Robert V. Ozment:

LOVE
IS THE
ANSWER

Robert V. Ozment

FLEMING H. REVELL COMPANY
OLD TAPPAN • NEW JERSEY

Scripture passages identified as PHILLIPS are from J. B. Phillips, *The New Testament in Modern English,* The Macmillan Company, 1965.

Scripture passages identified as MOFFATT are from James Moffatt, *The Bible: A New Translation,* Harper & Row, Publishers, Incorporated.

All other Scripture passages are from *The King James Version of the Bible.*

The poem by Ella Wheeler Wilcox is used by permission of Rand Mc-Nally & Company, Book Manufacturing Division.

The verse from "Just When I Need Him Most" is by Wm. Poole. Words and Music Copyright 1936 Renewal (Extended) The Rodeheaver Co., Owner. Used by permission.

"Tragedy of a Hunchback" and "There is Grief" are from the book *From My Window* by Frances Shumate, published by Vantage Press, New York. Used by permission.

*Dedicated to the loyal and faithful
members of Atlanta's First Methodist
Church whom it is
my privilege to serve*

Preface

One of the greatest needs of our generation is to learn to practice the love we see so clearly expressed in the life of our Lord. Love is the subject of the first and greatest commandment. Paul gives priority to love in his First Letter to the Corinthians: "In this life we have three great lasting qualities—faith, hope and love. But the greatest of them is love" (I CORINTHIANS 13:13, PHILLIPS). The gospel is saturated with God's love, and the cross is undeniable evidence of His unfathomable compassion.

Love is the answer to most of the baffling and perplexing problems that plague humanity. When we learn to apply in our daily lives the principle of love as taught *by,* and lived *in,* the life of Jesus, the clouds of bitterness and war will disappear from the horizon. Then we will see the sun of "peace on earth and good will toward men" sending its rays across our troubled world.

When the storms come, when we stand in the valley of despair and self-pity, when the future looks blurred, we need to direct our thoughts to the fact that God loves us. Such a startling truth will pierce any darkness that begins to descend upon us.

The Psalmist, while meditating on the greatness of God, exclaimed, "Thou hast beset me behind and before, and laid thine hand upon me" (PSALM 139:5, KJV). We do not use this little word "beset" very often. Actually, it means to "hem in," or "to surround." It is amazing to realize that we are "surrounded" or "hemmed in" by the love of God.

As the minister of a large urban church, I see a lot of people whose lives are tangled and whose problems are legion. I am fully convinced that most of their problems could be solved if they were only willing to practice the commandment of love. Love is the long, steep road God traveled from heaven to earth, and it is the same road we must travel from earth to heaven. Christian compassion is the bridge that spans the chasms of prejudice, envy, jealousy, and hate.

May this little volume help each one of us to live in the sunshine of God's love each passing day.

R.V.O.

Contents

Contents

LOVE IS THE ANSWER

1

When the Storms Come

There are several theological cloaks under which we may take cover when the storms of life descend, and there are many philosophical systems which have emerged; but basically man lives by one of two philosophies. Jesus expressed them in a parable in His Sermon on the Mount.

Some live by the philosophy that "today is all that matters," and they proceed to "make hay while the sun shines." I saw that philosophy expressed on the window of an automobile establishment a few months ago. A sign, painted in big colorful letters, stated: THERE AIN'T NO TOMORROW—THIS IS ALL THERE IS! Little wonder that we lose our perspective and sense of brotherhood. The man who believes only in today pushes God aside.

The other philosophy is based on faith. It can be expressed in this fashion: The man who gives life his best today will find the hand of God to guide him through each tomorrow. Such a man sees a silver thread running through the tapestry of life. It makes its way through each tomorrow, and doesn't end until it returns to the hand of God.

In the parable Jesus told, there are two men, and one does not recognize a great difference between them. Apparently, both were respectable. They lived in the same neighborhood and may have worked in the same office. They belonged to the same clubs and rode similar camels. To a casual observer, their houses were similar; it would be difficult, by observing, to determine which had the good foundation. (Once an electrician called to his

assistant, "Put your hand on one of those wires—feel anything?"
"No," replied the assistant. "Good, I wasn't sure which was which
—don't touch the other one or you'll drop dead," answered the
electrician.)

On the surface, the men in the parable appeared the same, but
actually there was a tremendous difference between them. One
was a very wise man who had built his house on a good foundation. He was very careful in choosing his material; every piece
of material was set with care. When the storms came and the
wind blew, that house stood the test.

The other man was foolish; he thought only of today. His only
wish was to satisfy his every desire. He nailed the decaying
boards of greed with the fragile nails of lust to the sagging
timbers of selfishness. Such a house will never stand the high
winds of adversity and the floods of sorrow that rage in every
life. Jesus gives us an account of the end of such a life: "And the
rain decended, and the floods came, and the winds blew, and
beat upon that house; and it fell: and great was the fall of it"
(MATTHEW 7:27).

Four thrilling truths can be grasped in this little parable. They
are not speculative truths; they are as certain as night and day.
They may be ignored, but they cannot be evaded:

(1) The first truth we discover is that God does not always
pay off on Saturday night. That is to say, we are neither rewarded for our virtues nor punished for our sins at the end of
each week or month.

Life is like a visit to the supermarket. You walk through aisles
which are well stocked with many good things to eat. You are
free to choose what you wish. You can take as little or as much
as you want. You must keep in mind that before the visit is
over, you must face the cashier. Before you pack your bags to
leave, you must pay for what you have taken. You face the
cashier alone, with what you have chosen. In many respects, life
is like that. You must face the Great Cashier before the journey
is over, and pay for the things you have taken from God's great
store of goods.

Very often a person will point out someone they know who lives life as he pleases, taking what he wants and rarely ever tipping his hat to God. "He is ruthless, vain and sinful. Yet, he seems to be getting along about as well as, if not better than, I," the conversation continues. "Yet, I try to be a Christian, and my troubles are more than I can number."

Almost every week I need to remind people that God neither rewards virtue with easy living, nor good deeds with an immunity from cruel blows or heavy loads. The Christian life is, in part, its own reward. We do not walk with God because He plucks from our hearts burdens we wish to discharge; we walk with God because He gives us strength to bear our burdens.

I am writing these lines on a beautiful day in October. I can see trees waving gently in the breeze. The landscape has been touched by the hand of God, and Mother Nature offers a magnificent scene that defies description. Every now and then I can see a leaf floating gently toward the ground. I am reminded of the law of gravitation. This law is constant, and without it man could not build skyscrapers or walk across a lawn. This is a natural law, and we never doubt its dependability.

God has a spiritual law which Moses expressed to Israel a long time ago: ". . . be sure your sin will find you out" (NUMBERS 32:23). Someday the real you will be revealed in the presence of God. Such a thought makes you shudder with the knowledge that the garments of pretense and pride will be removed. We all will stand in the presence of God, away from the false lights of flattery and compliments which are not applicable to our lives.

Jesus pointed out, in His parable of the two men building their houses, that the results of life will be revealed. The man who builds his house on a strong foundation will stand, and the man who builds his house on sand will fall.

(2)We may as well look for the storms, because they come to all of us. We are told that the Buddhists have a story about a mother who brings the lifeless body of her dead child to Buddha, requesting that he perform the miracle of resurrection and bring the child back to life. Buddha does not deny the request. First he asks the woman to find one family in which there is no sorrow. After a long and weary search, the woman returns; she has come back to withdraw her request. Sorrow, tragedy, pain, and suffering are universal. They come to men of every generation.

Bishop Gerald Kennedy tells a story about a professor who had finished his dinner at a campus cafeteria and was walking across the parking lot toward his home. He was overtaken by a student who appeared frightened. "I want to talk to you!" the student blurted out. "I can't eat, I can't sleep. I've just realized that one day I have to die!"

We cannot escape the conflicts of life. Edwin Lewis reminds us, in his little book *Christian Truth for Christian Living*, that "our world is much more a battleground than a playground. We are wise to remember that." When one enters through the door of birth and makes his way down the winding trail that finally brings him to the gate of death, he will encounter some of life's difficulties. All the roads of life wind through the valleys of sorrow and the Garden of Gethsemane.

Jesus never tried to obscure the risks involved in life. His invitation to discipleship was: ". . . take up the cross, and follow me" (MARK 10:21). In the parable Jesus told, He did not say, "*If* the storms come," or "The storms *may* come." He said, "And the rain descended, and the floods came, and the winds blew, and beat upon that house. . . ."

Some storms are sudden. They come without any warning. A few years ago, I lived in Lynn, Massachusetts, when a tornado struck about seventy miles away. It swept down into a sleeping town and killed dozens of people. There had been no warning. We have made great strides in forecasting weather conditions in this country. In spite of our scientific equipment, however, we cannot always tell with absolute precision what will happen.

Any religion that promises smooth sailing is deceptive and false. Bishop Gerald Kennedy suggests, in his book *The Parables*, "If the storm does not strike in one place, it will overtake us in another." Jesus never taught that to follow Him would offer us insurance against the hardships of life. He taught that to follow Him would give us assurance during the hardships.

(3) When the storms come, we must look within for our defense against them. I am not talking about human strength, but about divine strength. We have almost forgotten that our strength must be found in the spiritual realm if we are to face life confidently. We need to build braces of faith and trust within ourselves. We must develop a faith that believes in the goodness of God even when the shadows lengthen and the clouds of sorrow hide the bright stars that remind us of God's watchful care. We must trust God when the road is steep, our burdens are heavy, and the way is blurred.

In George Watts' famous picture "Hope," many people see only despair. They point to the bent figure, the lyre with all but one of the strings missing, and the poor woman who sits blindfolded in her defeat and misery. Some have suggested that the title might well be "Despair." What you see in the picture, however, represents the circumstances that surround the poor woman. The thing that makes her play the one remaining string is the hope in her heart. She does not draw strength from the pitiful conditions that surround her, but from the hope within her.

(4) The storms can be endured. God never gives us a task for which He does not provide the strength we need. He never permits life to place upon us an impossible burden. Jesus reminded us that ". . . with God all things are possible" (MARK 10:27).

When the storms come your way, what you do will be determined by what you believe. If, for example, you believe that God has been unfair to you, then you will likely become bitter toward God and move into a little room of self-pity. On the other hand, if you believe that God is behind life, and that Jesus Christ revealed unto us the true nature of God, then you will take your disappointments and sorrows and commit them to Him. This commitment may not stop the tears that flow from your eyes, but you will walk with a steady step and an unflinching confidence that when life on earth is finished, you will look into the face of a heavenly Father whose loving arms have supported you every step of the way.

Paul knew adversity. He was acquainted with the dingy prison cells of his day. Yet we hear him say, ". . . I know whom I have believed, and am persuaded that he is able to keep that which I have committed unto him . . ." (II TIMOTHY 1:12).

Now, the big question! What must we do in order to ride out and conquer the storms of life? Jesus gave us the answer to this question in His little parable: ". . . whosoever heareth these sayings of mine, and doeth them . . ." (MATTHEW 7:24). Whosoever heareth and doeth will be able to stand when the rains of sorrow descend, when the floods of trouble come, and when the winds of adversity blow.

But what did Jesus mean by ". . . these sayings of mine . . ."? He was just finishing the Sermon on the Mount. I find three golden threads winding through this sermon: (1) *love:* love God, and then love our neighbors as we love ourselves; (2) *forgiveness:* forgive others as well as receive the forgiveness of God; (3) *seeking first the Kingdom of God:* put God first in our lives, and other things will begin to fall into place.

If we can keep these sayings of our Lord, we can be triumphant in all of life. That is quite an order, but with His help we can do it.

2

Take the Lantern of Hope

A man drove a great distance to see me. He talked at length about the despair and futility that had settled in his soul. He outlined, in an articulate fashion, his intellectual doubts and skepticism. "You have related your doubts to me," I replied; "Now tell me about your faith and hope." He shook his head and answered, "I have no faith in God, and no hope for tomorrow." I did my best to push back the clouds of skepticism and show him God as revealed in the Gentle Galilean. Before my visitor left, I offered a prayer. I prayed that God would make him sensitive to the constant knock on the door of his heart, and give him the assurance of His presence.

I wanted the man to catch a glimpse of the truth expressed by the psalmist when he said, "Whither shall I go from thy spirit? or whither shall I flee from thy presence? If I ascend up into heaven, thou art there: if I make my bed in hell, behold, thou art there. If I take the wings of the morning, and dwell in the uttermost parts of the sea; Even there shall thy hand lead me, and thy right hand shall hold me" (PSALM 139:7-10).

I assured my visitor of my prayers and urged him to listen for the voice of God to speak to his empty soul. I felt the sting of defeat in my heart as I watched him walk away. I sat down and wrote this sentence on a little card: "A man ceases to live when the lights of hope are extinguished in his soul."

If I could give to a man only one thing, I would give him hope. I am talking about the hope the psalmist wrote about when he said, "For in thee, O Lord, do I hope . . ." (PSALM 38:15). Hope in God is the only basis that exists for any worthwhile aspirations.

When hope is gone, a man quits trying. As long as he can see a flickering light from the lamp of hope, he is never completely defeated. Little wonder Samuel T. Coleridge wrote, "He is the best physician who is the most ingenious inspirer of hope." A woman will find the courage to keep her family together in spite of a drinking husband, as long as she can see a spark of hope. A man can tolerate the many faults of his wife, if he has hope in his heart. A salesman can live with many negative responses to his product, if the light of hope burns in his soul. The minister will return to his place of prayer and study to give his best to preparing sermons, as long as he keeps hope alive.

"What is the difference between faith and hope?" is a question many people have asked me. I submit to you that the two are somewhat alike. Faith is the power to believe. Ralph Waldo Emerson wrote, "All I have seen teaches me to trust the Creator for all I have not seen." Faith in God is the power to trust Him when reason and logic fail us. Hope, on the other hand, is the power that sustains us when we must wait during some dark night in life. One might say that hope is the extension of our faith when we bear heavy loads and walk through lonely valleys. Oliver Goldsmith wrote:

> Hope, like the gleaming taper's light
> Adorns and cheers our way;
> And still, as darker grows the night,
> Emits a brighter ray.

The Captivity, an Oratorio

Robert Louis Stevenson spent most of his life trying to escape the ravages of tuberculosis. One of his poems, "The Lamplighter," reflects a delightful boyhood dream. On winter evenings, Stevenson loved to watch the lamplighter make his way up and down the streets, lighting the lamps. The humble workman would move through the shadows of evening, climbing his ladder at every lamp post and leaving a glow that pierced the darkness. It was an indescribable thrill when the lamplighter would pause and give Stevenson a friendly smile. The poet wrote:

But I, when I am stronger and can choose what I'm to do,
O Leerie, I'll go round at night and light the lamps with you!

There is a lot of darkness in our world, some of it caused by hate and ignorance. Some of it grows out of our selfishness and stupidity. Still, some of the darkness has its source in our greed and complacency. Disappointment, trouble, and sorrow bring darkness to many hearts. It is up to us to light the darkness of hate and ignorance with lanterns of love and knowledge. Giving ourselves to God and living according to the teachings of the Master will dispel the darkness that has settled over our society.

Ask yourself these questions: What am I doing to help bring light to the dark places in the world? Have I offered a word of hope to the discouraged? Have I prayed for those who walk through the valley of grief? Have I offered to share the burden of one who bears a heavy load? The Christian church is dedicated to drive away the shadows of darkness caused by sin and injustice. We must point a frustrated world, which bears the stains of many sins, toward the Saviour who redeems and restores. We must show a weary humanity the way to the Christ who invites us to come into His presence and rest. Ours is the mountainous task of bringing a wounded society to the Great Physician who can heal its ugly sores.

As long as men have hope, they can reach their destiny. Most of us could say, with the ancient poet, "My hopes are not always realized." We know what it is like to hold a heart full of crushed dreams. Actually, the poet did not end his statement on such a negative note. He went on to say: ". . . but I always have hope." Such a philosophy will keep us from despair when the clouds of disappointment descend upon us.

That wise poet knew something about the realities of life. He was saying, "I do not always get my way in life, but in spite of that, I believe God will sustain me, and through His strength I can be triumphant." He was saying, "Regardless of the circumstances of life, I will trust in the goodness and wisdom of God." Is this not the same philosophy Jesus expressed in the Garden of Gethsemane? Calvary looked cruel and was only a few days away. Jesus prayed, "Father, all things are possible unto thee; take away this cup from me: nevertheless not what I will, but what thou wilt" (MARK 14:36). Jesus never intended to abandon His faith in God, even though He had to drink from the cup. He was not spared the cross, but He was filled with divine hope.

When I was preaching a series of services in a small town recently, a house burned to the ground. The newspaper printed the story of the disaster, and in the opening sentence the reporter wrote, ". . . nothing saved." I am sure most people knew what the reporter meant. He meant that all the household furniture was destroyed by the fire. Actually, he could have emphasized the things the fire did not destroy. For example, the story might have begun with this line: "Everything of importance was saved."

I happen to know that the three children were rescued, and the wife was unharmed. The good name of the family was not even scorched. They still had their health, and the husband still had his job. They kept their friends, and the compassion of their good neighbors was expressed in their offer to let the family stay in their homes until another house could be built. In the final analysis, the most important things were saved. Many valuable possessions were lost, but the family still had hope. They were already talking about rebuilding their home.

Before you allow the lights of hope to be extinguished in your life, take another look at the life of Christ. Let Him be your example in suffering and sorrow. Follow Christ when the way is hard and the opposition fierce. One could never conclude that

Jesus was victorious because His life was easy. On the contrary, it was Christ who met and mastered the hard experiences of life.

Jesus walked away from the carpenter's shop at the age of thirty, with a burning passion to save the entire suffering human race. He wanted to make, out of a divided humanity, a brotherhood of love where human lives and deeds would be a tribute to God. His dreams were noble and His purpose was pure.

During His early ministry, He drew large crowds and was accepted by many people. Then hostility against Him grew into open opposition. The crowds dwindled and the voices against Him spoke louder and more often. His own family failed to understand Him. His friends deserted Him, and about three years after He launched His public ministry with so much compassion, He faced the dark shadows of death. Humanity was far from a brotherhood, and Jesus' dreams seemed to crumble into dust. What then? Most of us would have abandoned our hopes, but not Christ. He walked to the cross with a steady step that expressed His undaunted faith and hope in God. James S. Stewart wrote, "He was quite sure that someday, in God's good time, it would all come gloriously true." He had a hope that did not fade in the face of so much suffering and so many trials. That is the hope we must have if we are to meet the trials of life successfully.

I have heard people say that Christ is a good example, but that it is impossible for us to follow His example. Let us not forget that, very often, when Jesus gave the invitation to discipleship, He would say, ". . . take up the cross, and follow me" (MARK 10:21). Read the Master's words to His frustrated disciples, "In the world ye shall have tribulation: but be of good cheer; I have overcome the world" (JOHN 16:33). What did Jesus mean? Perhaps He did not mean that you and I would be able to meet all the difficulties of life with the assurance and courage that were His. On the other hand, not even a pessimist could read defeat in His words. Whatever else Jesus may have meant, He was offering a word of hope to His disciples. He was saying, "Life may look impossible and hopeless at times, but I tell you, with God's help all things are possible."

Let us trust Him when the way is dark and the load is heavy. When we face the dark shadows of Gethsemane, or the rugged slopes of Calvary, or the burning fires of criticism, let us remember that the same divine power that was our Lord's is available to us. When we stumble through deserts of sorrow or walk on the brink of temptation, we must look for the footprints of the Master and walk in them.

Almost two hundred years ago, a young man worked at his cobbler's bench, repairing shoes. More than anything else, he wanted his life to count for God. Mending shoes was an honorable job, but the cobbler felt that God had greater work for him to do. He became a Baptist minister, and on May 31, 1792, William Cary, the former cobbler, preached a sermon that has become famous for these words: "Expect great things from God. Attempt great things for God." Then, in 1793, he sailed to India and gave his life as a missionary. No person can expect great things from God or attempt great things for God unless he keeps the light of hope burning in his heart.

A man must believe three things if he is to walk through life with the lantern of hope in his hand:

(1) He must believe that God is the creative force behind this marvelous universe. This universe, with its precision and order, did not emerge from a sea of chaos and nothingness. It is the work of a power that defies description, and a mind that is unfathomable. The person who is so blind that he is unable to see God's intelligence in the orderliness of the universe will never know the hope that leaps in the heart of one who is more sensitive to the mind of God.

(2) Not only must a person believe that God is the Creator, but he must also believe that God is the sustaining force in His creation. Unless we are able to feel the gentle touch of God's hand upon us, we are headed toward the valley of hopelessness where defeat and misery are the order of the day. You and I are neither wise nor strong enough to face life victoriously with mere human wisdom and strength.

(3) A man must believe that God waits in each tomorrow.

He can face tomorrow with an unwavering hope if he believes that God stands in the shadows, guarding His own. A man cannot march with a steady step unless he expects to find love, joy, and goodness in tomorrow. No one can walk triumphantly into a sea of nothingness.

When you feel alone, remember that you are still in the presence of the King. When you see God revealed in Jesus Christ, you find fresh hope and new courage. Jesus gave us a verbal picture of God as a Good Shepherd. In Jesus' day, a good shepherd would not turn his sheep out of the fold and let them hunt green pastures while he engaged himself with other work. The shepherd never said to the sheep, "Now you are on your own. Go out and find tender grass and fresh water. You'll have to watch out for yourself, because I have other duties that demand my attention." Not at all! The good shepherd would find the green pastures and guard the sheep from any impending danger.

After the resurrection, Jesus gave His disciples the Great Commission, their greatest challenge: "Go ye therefore, and teach all nations, baptizing them in the name of the Father, and of the Son, and of the Holy Ghost: Teaching them to observe all things whatsoever I have commanded you . . ." (MATTHEW 28:19-20). That was a challenge because Jesus had just struggled up Golgotha to the cross for preaching the gospel He was asking them to preach. There was still bitterness and hostility toward those who were close to Jesus. Only a few days before, the disciples had hidden behind locked doors.

Not only did Jesus give them a great challenge, but He also gave them a great hope. Like the Good Commander, He did not send them alone into the battlefields of evil. ". . . lo, I am with you alway . . ." (MATTHEW 28:20). That is a different picture.

When my son Randall was about six years old, we were walking from my study to the house. It was a dark night and we walked hand in hand. On the way, I noticed the door to the toolhouse had been left open. It was not more than fifty feet away, but the tall pines cast black shadows all around. "Go close the door to the toolhouse," I suggested; "I will wait here." Randall took two steps toward the toolhouse, and a dog down the street let out an awful yell. Randall jumped back and said, "I don't want to go." "There isn't any reason to be afraid," I urged him; "Anyway, I can see you all the way." As quick as a flash, he answered, "If you'll go with me, I won't be afraid." It must have been a great source of comfort and courage when the disciples heard that last phrase, "I am with you alway."

I am positive God did not intend for me to be a poet. I just don't have the ability to make the lines come out right. But I did write a few lines after talking to a lovely lady who had known many disappointments. Her shoulders were stooped and her heart had borne many burdens, but her faith was inspiring. I went back to my desk, and wrote:

Sometimes the road is rough and the way is steep,
 But no matter how stony the path, or how dark the night,
Let us always remember we're the Good Shepherd's sheep
 And we move and live in the Good Shepherd's sight.

So the disciples went out into a hostile world with the hope that came from the knowledge that God walked with them. Let us move out with that same hope.

When life becomes a burdensome task instead of a thrilling adventure, there is hope. Some months ago, I visited a man in a hospital. He had endured great pain, and the marks of sleepless nights and excruciating pain were evident in his face. "I didn't know I would come this way," he said. He expressed a universal truth. None of us ever expect to lift the heavy burdens of life, but all of us will.

I walked through a lovely rose garden last summer. Stately roses of every color and variety waved gently in the summer breeze. The rose has been lavishly blessed with sweet perfume as well as beauty, which cannot be adequately described with all the flowing adjectives at our command. Then, one cold, blustery day in January, I took a hurried walk through the same rose garden. What a transition! A rose garden in January is a pretty horrible sight. You see ugly stalks wearing their garments of unsightly thorns. They stand like little soldiers waiting for a command to march out of winter into spring.

For many of us, life is like that. We face the hard days of winter when we see only the thorns and feel the sharp edges of the gardener's shears. Life becomes more of a strain and less of an adventure. But remember, God's help is available, and spring always follows winter.

Take the advice of the psalmist: "Cast thy burden upon the Lord, and he shall sustain thee: he shall never suffer the righteous to be moved" (PSALM 55:22). The first thing the psalmist suggests, when our burdens are heavy, is to cast them upon the Lord. He knew the foolishness of struggling up the path of life alone. Paul advised us to let our requests be made known to God. Jesus encouraged men to ask, seek, and knock. He assured us that our asking would get results, and our seeking would lead to fulfillment, and our knocking would open doors that were closed.

Then the psalmist said, ". . . he shall sustain thee. . . ." He did not indicate that God would lift our burdens. He did not say that God would wipe away all our tears and relieve our pain. He promised only that God would sustain us.

Look up that word *sustain*. Find out what it means. It means "to provide for," or "to give support." When we cast our burdens upon the Lord, we find a fresh supply of strength. He supports us with His strength and presence.

Finally, the psalmist wrote, ". . . he shall never suffer the righteous to be moved." God does not always take His wounded soldiers out of the battle, but He will never suffer them to be defeated. Those who are faithful to His commands shall win the victory. When the battle is raging, do not think for one moment that God has forsaken you. Do not become fearful and desert your post. God is near, and His grace is adequate.

God never sends us into a valley from which there is no escape. He never sends us up a mountain that cannot be climbed. He never places a chasm before us which we cannot span. Life is never impossible, because God refuses to deceive us.

The man who feels the touch of God's hand today will not be afraid of tomorrow. Tomorrow may bring its disappointments, but God will be near to steady him. There may be some unexpected sorrows in tomorrow, but once a man walks with God, he knows that His presence is all he needs to face tomorrow unafraid.

When God called Moses to lead the children of Israel out of Egypt, Moses made a number of excuses. He reminded God that he had many handicaps. Moses told God that he could not speak very well; he was certain that the Hebrews would not listen to him. "Who am I, that I should go unto Pharaoh, and that I should bring forth the children of Israel out of Egypt?" (EXODUS 3:11). Had it been left up to Moses, he would have preferred to live a shepherd's life.

God assured Moses that He would walk with him and that his efforts would not fail. Finally, Moses consented to go. He faced many trials and tribulations, but they neither made him afraid nor dimmed his faith. Near the end of his earthly journey, he turned his place of leadership over to Joshua. It had been a long, hard journey, but Moses' words were full of courage and his heart was steadfast. He said, "Be strong and of a good courage, fear not, nor be afraid: ... for the Lord thy God, he it is that doth go with thee; he will not fail thee, nor forsake thee" (DEUTERONOMY 31:6). What made the difference in Moses? It was his walk with God.

Even in death, the Christian can hear the bells of hope ringing clear and loud. Death is always a time of sorrow, but it is also a time of hope. If the resurrection is not true, then Jesus Christ has deceived us. I, for one, will trust the Master, and my daily song will always be, "I am the resurrection, and the life: he that believeth in me, though he were dead, yet shall he live" (JOHN 11:25).

Just recently, in one of our church papers, I was reading a memorial service for some of God's faithful servants. At the end of the service, the author had written a prayer. The typesetter had made a mistake. The prayer began: "Our dead Heavenly

Father. . . ." It should have read, "Our *dear* Heavenly Father.
. . ." That one little letter makes the difference between despair
and hope.

Charles Warner ended a poem with these words:

And death's not the end 'neath the cold, black sod—
'Tis the inn by the road on the way to God.

The tears of sorrow are less stinging when one comes to realize
the great truth of the resurrection. The cross could not stop our
Master; the grave could not hold Him. He lives, and because He
lives, the bells of hope ring out sweet music to sorrowing
hearts.

The Christian is never without hope. Read the words of Paul,
the spiritual giant, expressing his magnanimous faith: "We are
troubled on every side, yet not distressed; we are perplexed, but
not in despair; Persecuted, but not forsaken; cast down, but not
destroyed" (II CORINTHIANS 4:8-9). Paul was reminding us that
God never sends us down a dead-end street. In spite of the hardships Paul endured, none of them ever brought him to defeat,
because the power of God sustained him. Paul was saying, "I
have known trouble, but I have never given up. I have been
perplexed, but I have always had hope. I have been persecuted,
but through all of it, I have felt the hand of God. I have been cast
down, but never defeated." When our human eyes fail to see the
light of hope, God's long arm of love surrounds us. Paul knew
what it meant to be forsaken by his friends, but he never had the
experience of being forsaken by his Father. ". . . the Lord stood
with me," he wrote (II TIMOTHY 4:17).

Recently I called on a man who had suffered a severe heart
attack. For almost two weeks, he had been flat on his back. It
looked as if he would be there for several more weeks. It is
mighty easy to get discouraged while one is sick. I sat in the
man's room for a few minutes and offered a prayer. As I left, I
remarked, "Keep your chin up!" He replied, "I am helpless—but
not without hope." There may be times when you and I shall feel

helpless, but if we walk with God we shall never be without hope.

There is a story about an old man who lived in a desert wasteland of Arizona. He had the only good well of water in the entire area. Each evening, he would light his lantern and hang it high on a post outside his cabin. Some thought the old man was crazy to waste his precious oil. Nevertheless, night after night, the little lantern sent its ray of light out into the darkness.

Late one night, in the terrible heat of summer, the friendly old man heard a faint knock at the cabin door. He opened the door to find a traveler almost dead for want of water. The exhausted man had seen the glimmer of light from a distance and, with his last ounce of energy, had made his way toward it in the hope of finding water. A man's life was saved because an old man cared enough to light a lantern every night so that one who might be lost could find his way.

Almost two thousand years ago, God lit His lantern. It shines across the centuries, offering hope to all who will come and rest in its light. The cross is God's lantern and it shines along the path you are traveling. Do you have a sorrow that you cannot bear alone? Take it to the Christ of Calvary. Do you have some stains of sin that need cleansing? Take them to the Christ of Calvary. Do you have dreams that lie crushed, and hopes that are shattered? Take them to the Christ of Calvary. God's lantern will guide you safely through life, and it never, never goes out.

3

Lonely, But Not Alone

The streets of every large city in the world are crowded with lonely people. Atlanta, the city in which I live, is a city of beautiful homes, fine hospitals, expanding industry, stately churches, as well as honored universities and colleges. One might think that such a place would insure bliss and happiness. There are unnumbered thousands who know the folly of such a conclusion. A parade of the lonely and frustrated people of any great city would include marching feet from every social status. You would see the rich and poor, the ignorant and educated, the young and old in such a parade.

Why are people lonely? Many people become lonely and unhappy because of a distorted sense of values. Are we not guilty of thinking that inner happiness comes from the glitter of material things? A man said to me recently, "I'm about as miserable as a man can get, and yet I can find no reason for my unhappiness." Then he told me about his lovely wife and fine children. He talked about his success in the business world and his host of friends. He owns a summer home and travels extensively. "I've been everywhere," he said, "and done everything, and still life is empty." I told him that he had placed the emphasis on the wrong things in life. It is not enough to make money and be successful in the business world. Life is too big to be satisfied with superficial things. Then I said, "You may not like what I'm going to say, but I believe it ought to be said. You have been everywhere except to visit God, and you've done everything except to give your heart to Him. You must do this before you will ever be genuinely happy."

Human beings are never happy because of that which surrounds them, but because of that which lives within them. Paul said, "For to me to live is Christ . . ." (PHILIPPIANS 1:21). Paul was saying two very important things in that phrase: (1) he had completely dedicated his life to Christ; and (2) in his dedication he had found the purpose of life, and with Christ he could reach the destiny for which he was created.

Our business is to follow God, and if we are faithful He will eventually bring us to that Eternal City where the sorrows and frustrations of life are lost in the sea of yesterday. It is true that God may lead us down some strange paths, but let us have no fear, because His Way is always the best. Joshua Liebman, in his book *Peace of Mind,* wrote: "When we enter the tunnel of darkness, we forget that there is an exit as well as an entrance, and that we can come out into the light again. . . . It is a brief tunnel of darkness carved into the mountain of light."

Some months ago, I preached the funeral of a very gracious woman. She had loved the church and was devoted to her husband. The couple had been married many years, and parting was difficult. "I just can't give her up! I just can't go on without her!" the husband kept saying over and over. He was having a hard time adjusting to life without his wife, but he knew that he must try. I visited with him for a few minutes some months after the funeral. Before I left, he said, "This has been a long, dark night, but I believe I see the dawn breaking. Two things have sustained me," he continued; "first, my faith in a good God who always works for the best interest of His children. I know my wife is waiting for me on the shores of eternity. Then, I cannot help but remember that while life here will never be the same again, it never would have been what it is without the many wonderful years we spent together."

Keep in mind that no depression is a permanent state of life. The night may be dark and long, but the dawn is sure to come. I like that little story about the man who asked the wise old man to quote his favorite passage in the Bible. The old man replied, "My favorite passage is this: 'And it came to pass . . .' " (LUKE 18:35). The man waited patiently for the rest of the verse, and then asked, "Tell me the rest of it." The wise old man replied, "That is all of it." He went on to explain, "You see, I have had many troubles during my life, but none of them ever stayed for long. That is the reason I say my favorite passage is, 'And it came to pass.' Troubles will come, but they will also pass away." When the clouds of despair descend upon us, we must keep in mind that they are only temporarily present. We need not entertain them for very long.

Some people permit their circumstances to determine their attitude toward life. That is a very dangerous guide. Instead of permitting your outward circumstances to determine your whole attitude toward life, let your faith in God help you to meet and master your circumstances. You will never be utterly defeated if you develop a strong faith in God. I am not talking about simply believing that God exists; your faith must be deeper and stronger than that. You must believe in a God of perfect love and wisdom. You must trust God completely. It is mighty important that you believe in a God who loves you and whose actions reflect His perfect wisdom.

Katharine Hathaway's father was a professor at Boston University. When Katharine was five years of age, she was stricken with a spinal disease that took her off the playground and placed her in a bed of pain. For the next ten years of her life she lay on her back. She was strapped on a sloping board and her head was kept from sinking onto her chest by means of a leather halter. As a little girl, she had often watched a hunchbacked locksmith who came to her house to repair locks. He seemed to live in a world of his own, seldom looking up from his work.

After ten years of living in her strange world, Katharine was able to get up, and painfully she learned to walk again. Finally, when alone, she got up enough courage to look at herself in the mirror. She was a hunchback, not very attractive. As she looked in the mirror, she said, "That person in the mirror couldn't be me." Adjusting to a new life was not easy. She was often depressed and unhappy. Determined that misfortune would not defeat her, she grasped one truth that all of us need to know. She knew that her mind could grow independently of the size and shape of her body. She thought of the body much as she thought of a house. The body is the place where the real person lives, much as a house is a place where people live. The body is not really important. The person who lives in the body is important.

Katharine Hathaway may not shake the foundations of society, but she has learned to face life honestly and to believe in a God who can be trusted. Somehow, I believe she satisfied God by the way she faced the hard circumstances of her life.

Helen Keller wrote, "Dark as my path may seem to others, I carry a magic light in my heart. Faith, the spiritual strong searchlight, illumines the way and, although doubts lurk in the shadows, I walk unafraid toward the Enchanted Wood where the foliage is always green, where joy abides, where nightingales nest and sing, and where life and earth are one in the presence of the Lord."

The secret of dealing with the trials of life is the little magic light of faith we carry in our hearts. Carry faith with you and, while the clouds of despair may descend upon you, the way will never be so dark that you cannot see how to take the next step. The next step is really the most important step that any of us needs to take now. Let us not brood about tomorrow; rather let us make the most of the opportunities and challenges of today.

In the closing paragraph of Pierre van Passen's book *Days of Our Years*, he writes, "However dark the immediate future, all is not lost. Humanity will live by the faith and the hope . . . of the men who say: 'Nevertheless and in spite of everything, and whatever may come, I believe.'"

What you believe about God and life will mean the difference between defeat and victory. If, in spite of everything, you believe that God stands behind life and is the Sovereign Ruler of the universe, you will be triumphant. If you feel that life is a mere accident and that there is no compassion at the heart of this world, you will be crushed by both the circumstances that surround you and your lack of faith within.

When the lights of faith grow dim and the soul is burdened with heavy loads, you would do well to remember some of the lessons that history teaches us. Often, you may begin to think that God has singled you out, and that you walk the stony path alone. When you are lonely and frustrated, remember these four things:

(1) Never say, "God doesn't love me." When you were born, God showered His love upon you, and nothing can change that love. Paul wrote, "For I am persuaded, that . . . [nothing] shall be able to separate us from the love of God, which is in Christ Jesus our Lord" (ROMANS 8:38-39).

I have read a lot of clever phrases and clichés that may soothe some troubled souls, but they offer little comfort to me. For example, some say, "God gives the heaviest load to those He loves the most." I cannot accept that. I remember when I was a lad helping my father cut wood. He always said, "Now, son, let me take the heavier end." That is very much like God: He takes the heavier end. Oscar Wilde wrote, "Where there is sorrow, there is holy ground." Sorrow does not necessarily draw us closer to God; it sometimes causes us to turn our backs on God. I am inclined to agree with Plato when he said, "Of our troubles we must seek some other cause than God."

You do not love your children less when they are sick or in trouble. Actually, you draw close to them and stand ready to do anything possible to help them. God is like that. When we are in trouble, He stands near us to do what He can to help us. Rev. William Poole expressed this in his song, "Just When I Need Him Most":

> Just when I need Him, Jesus is Near,
> Just when I falter, just when I fear;
> Ready to help me, ready to cheer,
> Just when I need Him most.

God walks with us from the beginning of the journey to the gates of eternity. When we are ready to acknowledge His presence and live according to His wishes, we begin to live triumphantly. David, in the Twenty-third Psalm, wrote, "The Lord is my shepherd; I shall not want" (v. 1). What did David mean? He meant that as long as we follow the Good Shepherd, we shall never lack the refreshing water of divine love. God shall lead us in green pastures where we shall find the spiritual strength to meet every situation with faith and courage. When the soul needs to be restored, God shall forgive us. When we face the dark valleys of life, we need not be afraid because God's hand shall steady us. When our hearts are broken and the lights of joy have been all but extinguished by the rains of sorrow, God shall stand by us to comfort and strengthen us. David was saying, "The only way you can reach your destiny is to walk with God." The journey through life may not be all you want it to be, but that does not mean that God has forsaken you. Write these three things upon your heart: (1) God walks with us; (2) God loves us; (3) with God, we can be triumphant.

(2) When you compare your disappointments and trials to those our Lord knew, you must conclude that yours are rather insignificant. Jesus was a perfect Man. By that, I mean that Jesus never disobeyed His Father. He loved God with all His heart, soul, mind, and strength. He was constantly praying that God would guide Him safely through temptations. More than anything else, Jesus wanted to be sure He marched by divine music rather than the music of the world. There were many voices, but the voice He wanted most to hear was the voice of God.

In spite of His goodness, Jesus was troubled. What do you suppose He thought when He saw the shadow of the cross in His path? Do you suppose He said to Himself, "This isn't fair. I do not deserve this terrible experience. Why must I suffer so much when I have tried to live according to My Father's will?" One thing for sure, Jesus never accused God of being unfair. He never indicated that He would abandon His faith in God because of the suffering He had to endure on the cross. He was troubled, but never defeated. He suffered, but that drew Him closer to God. Jesus said, "Now is my soul troubled; and what shall I say? Father, save me from this hour: but for this cause came I unto this hour" (JOHN 12:27). He did not wish to turn back. When suffering is ours, let us march on, like Jesus, in faith, believing that somehow God will see us through. One thing I have observed, and that is that no person has ever been defeated who has kept his faith in God.

(3) Remember that you and I are not pioneers in facing the trials of life. The path over which we travel is stained from a host of bleeding feet that have passed the same way. The centuries of yesterday shout words of cheer and hope to those of us who march under the load of heavy burdens: "Don't give up! It isn't far to the top. Stop and rest awhile if you like, but never conclude that life is hopeless."

Norman Vincent Peale relates a story that took place during World War II. He was waiting in a railroad station, and when the train came in, the huge gateman let the soldiers pass through ahead of the civilians. A mother torn with grief hung onto her young soldier son who was about to leave. The boy, gently but firmly trying to free himself from his mother's grip, was obvious to all. He planted a kiss on his mother's cheek and hurried through the gate. As he passed out of sight, his mother leaned against an iron rail and sobbed bitterly.

The gateman, watching the woman closely, left his post and went over and spoke to her. Immediately a change came over her and she controlled her sobs, and the gateman helped her to a seat where she sat, calm and relaxed. As he walked away, the gateman said, "Now remember what I told you."

Dr. Peale was anxious to know what the gateman had said to the woman, so he engaged the man in conversation and asked what he had said. A little embarrassed, the gateman replied, "Well, it's this way. I saw that she had lost her grip, so I just went over and said to her, 'Listen, Mother, I know exactly how you feel. I have been through it myself. Lots of people have, but you have just got to forget these things. I don't mean that you are going to forget the boy, but you are going to forget your fears.' Then, I just added, 'Put your faith in God, and He will see both you and the boy through.' "

When the future is blurred, when the load is heavy and you seem to be alone, be quiet and let Christ speak to you. If you are sensitive to His voice, I am sure you will hear Him say, "Forget your fears. You are not alone in this. Put your faith in God, and He'll carry you through."

Robert Louis Stevenson wrote to a friend: "For fourteen years I have not had one day of real health. I have wakened sick and gone to bed weary, and yet I have done my work unflinchingly." Stevenson was saying, "Don't give up just because you don't get everything your way in life. In spite of your circumstances, you can achieve the goals God has set for your life."

Paul prayed that God would free him from the thorn in his flesh. That was a burden Paul did not wish to carry for the rest of his life. No doubt he felt that it would surely send him down to defeat. God did not remove the thorn in the flesh. He said to Paul, "My grace is sufficient for thee . . ." (II CORINTHIANS 12:9). You may be sure that God's grace is adequate for your every need.

(4) Whether you become a bitter person or a better person depends upon you. The way you react to life will send you either to the pits of despair or to the mountain tops of victory.

A letter came from a young woman who had lost her twenty-three-year-old husband after only a year of marriage. "We loved each other so deeply and my husband had so much to offer, I find it impossible to understand why he should die." Then she wrote, "But I believe that God does all things well, and to become bitter against God would only multiply my problems. I keep going in the faith that God loves me, and if I am faithful to Him, He will sustain me." What a grand attitude in the face of such a tragedy! I have never seen a person gain inner peace or spiritual strength from becoming bitter toward God. On the other hand, I have seen many people stagger up the hill of hard circumstances with a light of faith in their hands and a divine hand upon them to guide them through the tragedies they could not answer.

J. Wallace Hamilton tells a story about an old hermit who once lived in the mountains of Virginia. He was a wise man, gifted with a rare insight some are able to acquire "through close contact with nature and the God of the Garden." Some of the young boys of the village laughed at the old patriarch. "I know how we can fool him," one suggested. "I'll take a live bird," he continued, "and hold it in my hand and ask him what it is. When he answers, I'll ask, 'Is it dead or alive?' If he says it is dead, I'll let it fly away; if he says it is alive, I'll crush it." They went and found the old man standing in the door of his little hut. "Old man," said one of the boys, "I have a question for you. What do I have in my hand?" After carefully observing the boy's hand, the hermit replied, "Well, my son, it looks like a bird." "That's right," the boy replied, "but tell me, is it dead or alive?" The hermit looked for a moment and then answered, "It is as you will, my son."

It is as you will. You determine what you will do with your life. You and I may not choose the colors, but certainly we choose the pattern. No matter how many sorrows you know or how many disappointments you experience, how you face them is up to you. If you face them alone, you will fail; but if you face them with God, you will be triumphant.

4

Somebody Loves You

There is a grim scene in Maria Cummins' book *The Lamplighter*. Little Gerty, who is only eight years old, lives with Nan Grant. Gerty's mother had died in Nan Grant's house five years before, and little Gerty had been tolerated but never loved. Her daily diet, since her mother died, consisted of abuse and vulgar language. She was beaten, called an ugly, wicked child, told that no one loved her, and that she belonged to nobody.

Gerty loved to watch an old man light the street lamp in front of her house. To see the torch flicker in the wind, and to watch the old man hurry up the ladder and light the lamp, was a ray of joy in a desolate heart to which gladness was a stranger. The one bright spot in her long day was the moment when Trueman Flint, the lamplighter, came down the street, leaving in the shadows of night a flickering light on every lamp post.

One night, as darkness fell, Nan Grant sent Gerty down the alley for milk. She returned just in time to see Trueman Flint climbing the ladder. At the foot of the ladder she stood gazing intently, and as Trueman came down he bumped into Gerty, knocking her down and causing her to spill the milk. He turned quickly and picked her up. "What will your mammy say?" he asked. Then, looking into her sad face, he continued, "She won't be hard on such a mite as you are, will she? Cheer up, . . . I'll bring you something tomorrow that you'll like. . . ." Gerty brushed her ragged clothes, and said, "I was seeing you light the lamp and I ain't hurt a bit; but I wish I hadn't spilt the milk."

Just then Nan Grant came to the door and, seeing what had

happened, pulled Gerty into the house amidst blows and profane, brutal language. The lamplighter tried to appease her, but she slammed the door in his face.

The next night Gerty was waiting and the lamplighter was late, but quickly and carefully he pulled a tiny kitten out of his big coat pocket and gave it to Gerty. She showered the kitten with love and shared her meager food with it. For a month, she kept it hidden, but one cold night the kitten slipped into the house.

"Whose kitten is this?" Nan asked. "It's mine," Gerty replied. A few moments later, Gerty turned in time to see Nan Grant snatch the kitten from the table and throw it across the room. It landed with a splash in a pot of boiling water, and a few minutes later died in torture. Gerty, in a fit of anger, picked up a stick of wood and flung it at Nan and struck her in the head. The blood gushed from the wound, but Nan hardly felt the blow. She caught Gerty by the shoulder and pushed her out of the house, saying, "You'll never come in this door again," leaving her alone in the cold night.

The lamplighter came by a few minutes later and, finding the child crying and shivering in the cold, asked her the trouble. She told him the story and finally said, "She won't let me in! And I wouldn't go if she would." "Who won't let you in?" inquired Trueman Flint; "Your Mother?" "No! Nan Grant." "Who's Nan Grant?" "She's the wicked woman who drowned my kitten in boiling water." "But where's your mother?" "I haven't got one." "Who do you belong to, you poor little thing?" Trueman Flint asked. "Nobody; and I've no business anywhere."

This is the depth of human despair. This is the darkest night of the human soul. It is a desert where parched tongues and cracked lips find no water. No one had taught little Gerty that she was a child of God. No one had told her that Christ died for her sins and that He could light up the darkness within.

Life isn't worth living until you feel that you belong to somebody. You can't linger near Calvary without believing that your life does count. God's love for you becomes indescribable and undeserved.

I once held in my hand a note written by one who later placed a revolver to her temple and pulled the trigger. "Life holds no meaning for me. I see no reason why I should hang onto broken dreams and hopes that will never come true. What's left?" she wrote, moments before she pulled the trigger.

The woman lived in a beautiful house. Her bank account was bulging with money. Her closets were filled with lovely clothes. A new automobile was parked in her garage. She had friends by the score. Her life had been filled with gay parties and social activities. A desert had gradually filled her soul, and darkness hid the decent lights that give meaning to life. "She must have been mentally sick," some said. I am sure they were correct. When you empty life of compassion for others and concern for a starving world, a part of your soul becomes numb. When our little concerns hide the hurts of others, we become lonely and empty, and self-pity becomes our daily diet.

"What's left?" she had asked. There were thousands of people living in her city who needed shoes for bare feet, clothes for skinny backs, and food for empty stomachs. There were hundreds of hospital rooms filled with sick people who needed someone to come by for a visit. There were many little girls who needed someone to teach them how to cope with the problems they faced. That's not all! "What's left?" There is God. There is always God. He may not be all you want, but He is all you need in order to find meaning in life and walk triumphantly through the inevitable experiences that come your way.

We all want to be important and achieve distinction. There is, in most of us, a burning desire to lead the parade. Alfred Adler, one of the fathers of modern psychiatry, points out that the dominant impulse in human nature is the desire to be somebody, the wish to be significant.

We are skilled in our ability to gain attention. We are clever when it comes to methods that usher us to the center of the stage. Some seek attention by sitting on flagpoles. Others cross the Atlantic in a small boat. Still others wear loud clothes, and some turn to gossip. A few become criminals, and others let their hair grow long like the Beatles.

Praise never makes us despondent. Compliments never make us sad, even when we know we do not deserve them. Jesus spent very little time talking about the faults of people. He did not dwell on their sins, but on God's forgiveness. He challenged humanity to stand tall, and pointed out what we could become with God's help.

Some months ago, I was asked to visit a patient in one of our hospitals. She was a very sick woman, but was able to carry on a conversation. She complimented me more than I deserved. She said, "I've been to your church, and you are the best preacher I have ever heard. I've read some of your books, and you are a great author. You are the sweetest, kindest person in the world. You are a very handsome man." About that time her special nurse came in. I offered a prayer and left the room. The nurse very kindly walked to the door with me. She gently closed the door, following me into the corridor, and said, "Dr. Ozment, I don't know what the patient might have told you, but she is gradually losing her mind, so don't believe anything she said." "She carried on a perfectly grand conversation," I replied, "and I believe every word she said."

The advertising world appeals to our desire to be important. Ads tell us we should drink a certain brand of liquor if we want distinction. They advise us to smoke a certain cigarette if we want to be popular. They remind us to wear a certain make of clothes if we want to achieve success. We must drive a certain car if we want others to be envious of us. Ads even tell us what kind of deodorant to use if we want to keep our friends; they warn us about being half-safe, whereas, if we use a certain brand, we are supposed to be safe for twenty-four hours. When I was a lad, we took a bath that would last a week. If you take a bath with a good strong soap, it will still last you a long time.

Ego that is untamed or undirected can be vicious. Carl Sandburg, in his biography *Abraham Lincoln*, had this to say about John Wilkes Booth, the man who shot Lincoln: "He did what he pleased and took what he wanted. . . . They saw vanity grown in him—vague, dark, personal motives . . . to be feared; projects and purposes vast with sick desire, dizzy with ego." Has history concluded that a giant tree was felled in the forest of civilization by the hand of one sick with ego?

There isn't anything wrong with our desire to be somebody. Evil enters when we push others down in order to push ourselves up. On the other hand, it is wrong to be content to be a nobody.

A bishop in the Methodist Church, examining a group of young candidates for the ministry, asked if they had any desire for preeminence in their work. All of them answered in great humility that they had none. "Well," the bishop said, "you are a sorry lot, all of you." The young men stood embarrassed, and the bishop continued by reminding them that no person ever fired the ambitions of men like the Master. It was Jesus, more than any other person, who made little people feel big and important.

If I owned a bank, I wouldn't hire a man who didn't want to be president of the bank. If I owned a department store, I wouldn't hire a person who didn't want to be manager. Reality never outruns our dreams. You may never attain all your dreams, but you will never go beyond them, either.

Remember that scene in the New Testament where James and John slipped around to ask Jesus for a special favor? "Give us the best places in the Kingdom," they requested. They wanted to lead the parade. There was no consideration given to Peter, Andrew, Thomas, and the rest. James and John wanted to sit one on the right and the other on the left side of the Master. Those were the places of honor in a monarch's court.

Did you ever stop to think about the response our Lord gave to that request? He did not rebuke His disciples, neither did He suggest that their ambition ought to be curbed. Jesus suggested that they did not know the depths of their request. Then He asked them two questions: ". . . can ye drink of the cup that I drink of? and be baptized with the baptism that I am baptized with?" (MARK 10:38). Jesus went on to explain that a place of honor could not be given away: it had to be earned.

J. Wallace Hamilton, writing about the incident, said that Jesus might have spoken in this fashion: "You want to be important.

You want to surpass others and be great among men. All right. You should! To be My disciples, you must! But be sure that it is real greatness you are after. Be sure it is a greatness worthy of God. If you would excel, excel in goodness. If you want to be first, be first in moral excellence."

Greatness is the fruit of Christian service. Jesus said, ". . . whosoever will be great among you, shall be your minister: And whosoever of you will be the chiefest, shall be servant of all" (MARK 10:43-44). He encouraged His disciples to be superior. ". . . what do ye more than others?" (MATTHEW 5:47). ". . . your righteousness shall exceed the righteousness of the scribes and Pharisees . . ." (MATTHEW 5:20).

The man who works for himself is selfish, but the man who works for others is a servant. An eloquent parade of great souls have dedicated themselves to a cause that reaches beyond personal ambition. Greatness is not achieved under the glitter of bright lights, but in the dark jungles of human need; in little rooms of dedication; in the halls of discipline, and in dimly lighted laboratories. Louis Pasteur is a star in the constellation of greatness. He often said, "In what way can I be of service to humanity? My time and energy belong to mankind." Albert Schweitzer could have lived in luxury, but he felt compelled to give himself to a suffering humanity. Madame Curie and her husband Pierre refused to exploit the commercial aspect of their discoveries. Concerning their research with radium, Madame Curie said, "If our discovery has a commercial future, that is an accident by which we must not profit. And radium is going to be of use in treating disease. . . . It is impossible to take advantage of that."

David Livingstone dedicated himself to lighting some lamps in darkest Africa. His greatness was found in the depth of his willingness to serve. Once he said, "I will place no value on anything I have or may possess, except in its relation to the Kingdom of God. Anything I have will be given, or kept, according as giving or keeping it shall I most promote the Kingdom of my Saviour."

What would Jesus say if He were to speak to us this day

concerning our desire to be somebody? He might say, "You are important. God made you to be great. Don't ever settle for less than true greatness."

When the people of France put Louis XVI and his queen to death, there was left a little boy, who, if the monarchy had stood, would have become Louis XVII. The boy was put into prison and surrounded with vicious and vulgar men. Their mission was to teach his mind to think vulgar thoughts and his lips to say evil and depraved things. When someone would suggest that he say a vulgar word, the boy would reply, "No, I will not say it. I was born to be a king."

You were born to be a king, and you can be. If you feel that your life does not count, read the words David wrote when he looked at God's great universe: "When I consider thy heavens, the work of thy fingers, the moon and the stars, which thou hast ordained; what is man, that thou art mindful of him? . . . For thou . . . hast crowned him with glory and honour" (PSALM 8:3-5). Read the words of Jesus: ". . . the very hairs of your head are all numbered" (MATTHEW 10:30).

Go back to Calvary and take another look. You'll come away with a new sense of appreciation of yourself. You are important. You can be somebody. Resolve to be great, but be sure your greatness is worthy of God.

5

Things We Do Not Deserve

When life knocks you down, you have three choices: (1) you can stay there; (2) you can turn to a bottle and try to forget your burdens and drown your sorrows; or (3) you can turn to God and ask Him to help you. When life falls apart, you decide whether you will stay in the valley, try to cover your hurts, or, with God's help, rise above them.

Let none of us march out into the world armed with the false notion that when a man is committed to God, he is placed under a protective shell that keeps him from the dark nights of life. Neither let us fortify ourselves with the idea that when life is dark, all we need to do is call upon God to remove the darkness. We cannot use God as men use radar to guide them around the storms of life; nor should we think of Him as a force that sends us, like spacecraft, above the frictions of earth. God is that power which makes life possible when it appears impossible. God doesn't lift us out of the bloody battles, but He keeps us steady during the struggle. God isn't a "problem solver," but He is that majestic force in life which enables us to live triumphantly in spite of the burdens we carry.

The question is not, How will I react if trials descend? The question is, How will I react *when* trials come? Hardships come with life, and we cannot live without suffering. Life has always been that way. Optimism, good fortune, and riches may make life easier when the hardships descend upon us, but they won't do away with the uninvited guests.

It was a dramatic moment when King Charles and Joan of Arc came face to face. The king questioned Joan about the voices she claimed to have heard. Irritated, the king suggested that the voices should have come to him, not to a mere subject. "I am king, not you," he proclaimed. With gentleness that reflected compassion, and with fortitude that expressed an undaunted faith, Joan replied, "They do come to you; but you do not hear them. If you prayed from your heart and listened, you would hear the voices as well as I do."

That's our problem! We are so busy nursing our hurts and bathing in our self-pity that we do not pray with our hearts and listen for God to speak to us. Often we denounce Him and display our lack of faith by asking, "Where is God?" But we neither offer our hand to God nor listen for His voice. Little wonder that we see only despair when life falls apart.

When a man faces God, he always leaves with a word of hope. God lights a candle of hope in every person who comes seeking help, no matter what the circumstances of that person's life. Jeremiah made excuses because he could not speak for the Lord when God called him. Then God said, "Be not afraid . . . for I am with thee . . ." (JEREMIAH 1:8). When God called Joshua to lead the Hebrews into the Promised Land, the task seemed beyond Joshua's strength. But Joshua went about his task with these wonderful promises ringing in his ears: ". . . I will not fail thee, nor forsake thee. Be strong and of a good courage . . ." (JOSHUA 1:5-6).

Remember that thrilling incident in the Old Testament when David went to the front lines to visit his brothers while Saul and his men were facing the Philistines? When the giant Goliath challenged anyone from the armies of Israel and defied the armies of God, something stirred within David. He offered to fight the giant. His brothers, as well as other soldiers, thought he was foolish. Even Saul tried to persuade young David that he didn't have a chance against the giant.

David convinced Saul that the Lord was with him and Saul

gave his consent for him to fight Goliath. With a simple sling and some carefully chosen stones, David conquered the giant. Previous to that simple act of courage and trust in God, the armies of Israel had trembled with fear each time the giant appeared. It's amazing what one can achieve when he anchors his faith in the goodness of God and walks with Him. It is also amazing to see how little are the things that make us stumble when we do not walk with God.

Frances Shumate does not like to think of herself as being handicapped, but the scars of cerebral palsy are evident. It has left its mark on her speech and her ability to get around, but her spirit has upon it the touch of the Master's hand. In her book *From My Window,* she writes about the tragedy of a hunchback:

One day he felt his hump dissolve until his spine stood straight.
Still he saw nothing but the patch of ground beneath his feet;
His only pleasure was retelling his catalogue of hate;
He'd let affliction twist his soul out of shape.

We can let bitterness twist our souls out of shape, seeing only the tears of today and never picturing in the mind the dawn of tomorrow. That is one way to face life when dreams are shattered and eager hopes are dashed to bits.

Frances Shumate refused to share the despair of the hunchback. Like all mortals, she felt the pain of disappointment when her dreams were crushed. In these words, she opened for a moment the door of her soul:

I know there is grief deeper than mine.
But, my grief is mine. It is my heart
Which feels the teeth of despair
Feeding bit by bit, tearing apart
The pattern I had dreamed.
May I be given the gift of grace
To welcome His choice for me,
To accept the pattern chosen to replace
The design of my desire.

When we learn to pray from a genuine heart for the grace of God which will enable us to accept that which cannot be changed, God will grant that strength and we will be well on our way to victory.

Life falls apart for many under the stress and strain of sickness. The achievements of the past are not sufficient to support us during a long period of sickness. When we are alone, we see wasted opportunities, selfish moves, and ugly deeds. It's easy to become a battered victim of despair.

A few months ago, I visited a man in a hospital who had been critically ill. For some days, he lay near the brink of death. During the long weeks of convalescence, he told me about his fears and hopes. He had spent most of one night considering this one question: "What if I don't make it?" He couldn't think of any achievements of which he was proud. Yet he thought of many deeds that brought shame to his heart.

"I have learned one thing from this sickness," he said. "I can tell you that the really important things are the things I have so often taken for granted. I didn't know before that I had been such a selfish man," he continued. He had been so busy making a living that he hardly knew his own children and they didn't really know him. He promised to be a better husband and father. He assured me that he wanted a place to serve in the church and something to do that would be an expression of his gratitude for the privilege of life.

In the New Testament we find a tender scene between Jesus and a woman who had been sick for twelve long years. She probably suffered from a chronic hemorrhage, which was not only embarrassing, but impoverishing and discouraging. She wanted so much to be well and had spent all her savings going from one physician to another. The primitive methods of the medical profession had failed to help her. Little was known about disease and few remedies ever brought relief in those days.

The woman had done all she knew how to do. Little hope was left. Now she must accept her poor health and learn to live with it. Then she heard about Jesus; His fame had spread quickly. He had healed others, and perhaps He could do something for her.

The news spread through Capernaum that Jesus had arrived. A crowd quickly gathered around Him. In that crowd many people held on to their fragile hopes. Among them was Jairus a leader of the synagogue; his little girl was dying and he begged Jesus to heal her. As the woman marched with the others through the dusty streets, hope leaped in her heart. How could she approach Jesus? He was in the company of important people; she was unclean. Blotches of blood could be seen on her clothing. "If I could only get close enough to Him," she thought to herself, "to touch the hem of His garment, I would be healed." Shyly, but with great determination, she stumbled through the crowd and gently touched His robe. "Only the Master can put my life together again," she thought. Jesus turned around and looked into her face and said, ". . . thy faith hath made thee whole . . ." (LUKE 8:48).

Life also falls apart when we lose our faith. The very first step on the ladder that leads to success is faith. Next are discipline, effort, patience, fortitude, and enthusiasm. You see, you can never conquer a problem until you believe it can be mastered. You can never achieve a goal until you are convinced that you can do it.

The disciples must have related to many who were filled with fear the incident that took place on the Sea of Galilee. The night was dark and the Master was asleep, when suddenly the placid little sea became a mountain of swirling and churning waves. Water splashed over the bow and it appeared that the boat would sink.

"Do you remember," Peter must have said to James, "we were tugging with all our might to keep the boat headed into the waves, and Jesus was sleeping peacefully?" "Yes," James probably replied, "and someone shouted, 'Master, don't You care if we perish?'" "Then," said Peter, "Jesus rebuked us for our fear and lack of faith. What a Man!" Peter mused, "He is the Son of God. There are no storms that He cannot calm. There are no lives that He cannot redeem. There are no problems that He cannot solve."

One theologian, writing about the question, "Master, don't you care if we perish?" remarked: "Stupid question." It is not stupid at all. When men are filled with fear, they lose their faith, and many a person has let that question fall from his lips. When the waters of earth threaten our happiness, or the happiness of those we love, it is not difficult to ask that same question.

I know a family who recently walked through one of life's darkest valleys. They hold today the broken pieces of what was a joyous dream. Slowly and painfully they are, under the guidance and help of God, putting life together again. The scars of sorrow will never be removed, but because of their faith in God they will find not only the strength to endure, but the joy of new adventure and the satisfaction of seeing new dreams fulfilled.

Faith overcomes other handicaps. Louis Pasteur was stricken with a paralytic stroke at forty-six. Some might have placed their tools on the shelf, but Pasteur worked on with an undaunted faith and unwavering courage. Helen Keller was both blind and deaf, and fear might have kept her locked in a tiny room until death. Instead she chose faith to produce the music by which she marched. Paul was the victim of a "thorn in the flesh," for which he prayed more than once that God would give him relief. His relief came in the form of God's strength to march on in spite of the "thorn in the flesh." Fear tells us that we do not count, that God does not need us. Faith proclaims, "You are important, and God can use you." When we follow faith, even a life that has been dashed to pieces can be put back together.

When we lose one who is close to us, life can fall apart. Sometimes the tears of Calvary hide from our minds the truth of Easter. As long as we focus our attention on the hurts of Calvary, we cannot hear the bells of Easter.

Three crosses silhouetted against a blue Syrian sky, with three men slowly but surely dying, made a grim scene. After almost six agonizing hours of suffering, the soldiers examined the three men. One soldier pierced Jesus' side with a spear. Before they marched back to their barracks, they were satisfied that Jesus was dead. His death was also reflected on the faces of the disciples. As the shadows lengthened, the disciples gazed at each other with puzzled looks of grief. "He's dead," said Simon Peter. Not only were the Roman authorities satisfied that Jesus was gone forever, but even the enemies of Jesus were happy to know that He would never get in their way again.

To take every possible precaution, the enemies of the Master asked Pilate to set a watch of soldiers at the tomb for at least three days. The haunting words of Jesus would not let them rest. "He said He would rise again after three days," they kept reminding one another. Pilate granted their request, saying: "Ye have a watch: go your way, make it as sure as ye can" (MATTHEW 27:65). The soldiers sealed the grave and left a detail to watch.

Then came the first day of the week. The Good News was announced. The truth of Easter was not accepted without evidence. The disciples at first refused to believe. Then Jesus appeared unto them and fresh hope filled their lives. Despair was changed to unwavering conviction. Fear was transformed, and humble disciples were filled with enthusiasm. Dr. George A. Buttrick said, "Why did these men suddenly rise from their bemoanings and, with light on their faces, fairly spring on the world with the message of a living Saviour for Whom they were willing to suffer any persecution?" The answer could be found only in the unequivocal knowledge that Christ was alive.

Do you believe the story of the resurrection? If you believe it and trust in God, the shattered pieces of a life broken by sorrow can be put together again. To believe this story will cause little flames of hope to leap from the cold gray ashes of sorrow.

If we do not believe it, then we must conclude that it is a shameful lie. God has deceived us and life is a big joke. If this story is not true, the Gentle Galilean was a filthy liar who painted pictures of hope on fragile parchments that disintegrate when the winds of reality blow. But the story is true, and death is merely the door that leads to the living room of God.

Finally, sin results in life falling apart. Evil separates us from God. It does not separate us from God's love any more than a wayward son could be separated from the love of a devoted mother. God has chosen to love us regardless of the thoughts of our minds, the deeds of our hands, and the attitudes of our hearts.

When life is torn apart by our ugly deeds, the only source of help is found in God. We cannot cover the stains of sin with good deeds. We cannot erase the sins of yesterday by making noble resolutions today. Our sins can be absolved only as we bring them to God in a spirit of penitence.

A few days after His triumphant march into Jerusalem, Jesus was with His disciples in the upper room. When the Master revealed the shocking news that one would betray Him, the disciples asked, with puzzled looks, "Lord, is it I?" (MATTHEW 26:22).

Before the last rays of a crimson horizon gave way to the darkness of night, Jesus said, "All ye shall be offended because of me this night . . ." (v. 31). There must have been a look of dismay on the faces of the disciples, and after a moment of silence Peter spoke: "Though all men shall be offended because of thee, yet will I never be offended" (v. 33). Jesus, in His gentle way, replied to Peter, ". . . before the cock crow, thou shalt deny me thrice" (v. 34). Peter fortified his first statement by saying, "Though I should die with thee, yet will I not deny thee" (v. 35).

From the upper room, Jesus and His disciples made their way through the shadows to the Garden. There He was arrested, and Peter was ready for the conflict. It was evident that Jesus was in danger of losing His life, and the hostility was greater than Peter had imagined. Before the morning sun chased the shadows away, Peter denied Jesus three times. Then, in the distance, Peter heard the cock crow. He had forgotten. The cock crowed again. He remembered! He slipped away and buried his face in his hands and wept.

"Look what an awful mess I've made!" Peter cried. "Will He forgive me? Can I ever look Him in the face? What can I do to make this up to Jesus?" Peter discovered that the past cannot be changed, but he soon learned that yesterday's deeds could be forgiven.

On the slopes of Galilee, Jesus came to His disciples, and when Peter recognized Him, he made a dash for Jesus. Peter had loved Him, had denied Him, and he still loved the Master. There in the freshness of a new day, Peter responded to the forgiveness of Jesus and went about feeding the sheep.

Have you ever loved Jesus? Have you ever denied Him? Do you still love Him? Will you come back, like Simon Peter, and let Christ cleanse and redeem you? The deeds of yesterday may be ugly and they may cause you to weep, but Christ can change all that. He will, if you give Him your permission.

6

Patch Up the Past

"What do you consider to be the main business of the Christian church?" someone asked me recently. Without hesitation, I replied: "The church exists for only one purpose, and that is to present the God we see so unmistakably in Jesus Christ to a staggering, weary, and undeserving humanity."

Our major business is not to promote little programs, nor to spend our time presenting lectures on current events sprinkled with irresistible charm. The church should not be a place where we come to be entertained, or to make friends. It must be a place where those who walk in the darkest night of life can see a star of hope and find spiritual strength. The church must keep the lights of hope lit. It is our task to bring people face to face with God, and thereby keep the torch of courage and faith burning bright. Let us proclaim the faith we see in the early Christians. They approached their task armed with the belief that nothing was impossible when God and man worked together.

When a man comes to church holding his shattered hopes and broken dreams, we can say, "Don't give up. All is not lost!" When a woman comes with her soul covered with the stains of many sins, we can shout, "God loves you and will forgive you! No person is beyond His redemption." When a young person brings a heart full of jagged disappointments, we can tell him about a God who knows the secrets of the heart, and whose grace is adequate for every situation.

I agree with James S. Stewart, the eminent Scottish preacher, who said, "Christianity, therefore, is right, absolutely right, when it refuses, in spite of a barrage of criticism, to be deflected from the one object for which it exists, which is to hold up Jesus." When we fail to lift up Jesus Christ, Christianity loses its power and is robbed of its vitality.

There are times when the sermon may pour out healing oil on wounded souls. At other times, the sermon may be compared to a painful operation without the comfort of a numbing anesthesia. Not only must we see our ugly deeds and filthy sins, but we need to experience the Christ who can cleanse us from our transgressions and transform us into new creatures.

No one would deny the fact that all of us need to see our faults; but I am convinced that a lot of preaching falls short. That is to say, it merely points out the evils of our society and fails to proclaim the message of redemption. Some preaching could be compared to a doctor's examination which clearly defines the disease but refuses to prescribe a cure.

It is not enough to be against hate; we must be for love. It is insufficient to make a stand against deceit; we must wave the flags of honesty. We fall short when we merely disdain a falsehood; we must crusade for truth. We cannot measure up to the standards of Christ by simply opposing infidelity; we must march in that army whose motto is "fidelity."

Some months ago, I received a letter from a woman in the Midwest. She thanked me for one of my books which she had just finished reading. Near the end of her letter was a sentence that stood out like a towering redwood in a pine thicket. It has caused me to consider very carefully the content of my own preaching. Here is the sentence: "Our preacher doesn't seem to be against anything and, furthermore, he isn't for very much." What a pity! The church cannot afford to drift with the crowd. It must be the compelling force which pulls man toward his destiny and the lighthouse by which men are guided safely through the storms.

After preparing each sermon, I ask myself some questions. Is there anything in here that would help guide a person who has lost the purpose of life back to God? Is there any grass in these words that will feed the hungry sheep? Is there a word of hope for the hopeless? Is there a bit of comfort for those who bear the burden of sorrow? Is there some courage for those who have lost their grip on life? Is there anything here that will offer a little light of faith to those who walk through the valley of uncertainty? Will this sermon bring people into the presence of God? I have come to believe that if a sermon does not bring worshipers face to face with God, the preacher's efforts are in vain and the congregation's time might well have been wasted.

Our preaching must not reside in the chasms of condemnation; it must climb the steep slopes of Calvary where the battle of good and evil was fought and won. Let us bring the weary to Christ, where they can find strength. Let us bring those who struggle under the weight of sin to Christ, where they can find release.

Jesus did not spend much of His time condemning the things that were wrong in His day. He talked about the God who could redeem and forgive. He was never without a word of hope and courage. Walk with Him over the dusty streets of Jericho and Capernaum. Travel with Him by the shores of Galilee. Ride with Him in the little boat across the sea. Listen to Him talk!

When Jesus heard the cry of blind Bartimaeus, He did not remind him of his sightless eyes and his bleak world of darkness. Jesus asked, "What do you want me to do for you?" Bartimaeus replied, "'Oh, master, let me see again!' 'Go on your way then,' returned Jesus, 'your faith has healed you'" (MARK 10:51-52, PHILLIPS).

One day as Jesus taught, a crowd gathered at the Mount of Olives. Very soon a poor woman was brought to Him and her sin was exposed to all who were near. She had been taken in adultery. Jesus did not condemn her. Why? Because her evil deed had condemned her already. He did not need to magnify the ugliness of it. She needed to be redeemed. Therefore, Jesus said unto her, ". . . go, and sin no more" (JOHN 8:11). Our churches are filled with spiritually sick people who are desperately searching for a prescription that will make them well again. The church has such a prescription.

I talk with a lot of people who are in trouble. No matter how dark and stormy the night, with God's help I can find a star of hope. In most counseling sessions I do little talking. Counseling is mostly listening. All the advice I ever offer is based on one principle: I believe in the sovereignty of God; God is behind life; He is the Ruler of the universe. You and I were created by Him and we never get—even for one moment—out of His sight. The gospel tells us many things, but one truth that rings loud and clear is this: Your life can be changed, or you can be transformed in your present situation.

I know a man who was indifferent to God and the church. As a matter of fact, he was bordering on cynicism and bitterness toward God. One day the storms of sickness descended upon him. He was rushed to a hospital. I went to see him and we had prayer together. He was sick for several months. We both prayed that God would spare him and make him well. Of course, we prayed, "Thy will be done. . . ." During the dragging days and long nights, he was forgiven of his sins and accepted Jesus as his Saviour. His whole attitude changed.

One day, when I entered his room, he talked very freely about his own situation. Among other things, he said, "This sickness has brought me to God. I only regret that I did not know Him before, so I could have lived for Him. I was afraid to die until I met God. The doctors have told me that I probably won't get well, but I am no longer afraid." God did not change the circumstances that surrounded that man's life, but He transformed the man in spite of his circumstances. If the wise God does not lift the load we bear, He will provide the inner strength we need to keep walking without ever falling.

Have you ever heard of Death Valley, California? It borders on the State of Nevada, and is the lowest, hottest, and driest land in the United States. Normally, there are only a few inches of rainfall in this valley each year, not enough for the plants to grow. While the land is not entirely lifeless, it is ordinarily a desolate valley of sand dunes. Ironically, only eighty miles away stands the awe-inspiring Mount Whitney, which is the highest point in the United States.

During the month of May, 1930, rain fell in Death Valley for nineteen consecutive days. During those days, seeds that must have been dormant for years sprang to life, and parts of the valley became a carpet of beautiful wild flowers. Buttercups, Indian paintbrush, poppies, larkspur, and other flowers transformed the ugly, dry desert into a gorgeous flower garden. It was reported that a hundred varieties of flowers were found within a half hour in one small area.

Many of us live in a desert without faith or hope. When we put our faith in God and let Him occupy the center of our lives, the dull sand dunes of the soul are transformed into a garden of beauty. The flowers of hope and courage bloom everywhere, and suddenly the gray yesterdays are changes into bright tomorrows.

H. G. Wells, in his book *God the Invisible King*, wrote, "Religion is the first thing and the last thing, and until a man has found God, he begins at no beginning; he works to no end." It is quite evident that a host of people do not believe the truth of that profound statement. The man who tries to manage his life without the help of God is like a captain trying to bring his ship to harbor without either an engine or a rudder.

We live in a world where our sense of values has become confused. Many of us have grown to be selfish and cruel. Money has become more important than morality. Position, for some, has become more desirable than intergrity. Others would rather achieve power than moral stature.

Our society reminds me of the story about several boys who broke into a department store and for several hours changed the price tags on the merchandise. They put three-dollar price tags on five-thousand-dollar mink coats, and five-thousand-dollar tags on three-dollar handbags. The clerks discovered one-dollar price tags on two-hundred-dollar suits, and two-hundred-dollar tags on one-dollar ties.

I once noticed a woman who attended church every Sunday and sat in the same seat. She was not a member of the church and never participated in other activities of the church, but she was always in her place when the worship service began. One day I had an opportunity to visit with her, and I asked her why she felt it necessary to attend church every Sunday. I told her that she came more faithfully than some of those who belonged to the church. She was a very humble woman and one who loved God. She said, "I carry many burdens which most people do not know about. I work hard all week and the nature of my work often causes me to become depressed. I come to church each week in order to give God a chance to speak to me. I get my empty buckets of hope and faith filled in church each Sunday, and God sends me back to my work with all the strength I need to carry my burdens.

Dr. Pierce Harris was for twenty-five years pastor of Atlanta's First Methodist Church. One day a member said to him, "I first came to this church because I liked you. Then I came for a while because I enjoyed the church and the people who come here. Now I come to church because I love God." To fill empty hearts, and to teach people to love God and follow His teachings ought to be the goals of every church.

The Christian church must become like a lighted torch in a weary world of doubt and frustration. I remember a young minister who called and wanted to see me. He was disturbed about his Christian faith. "I'm afraid I will be a failure as a minister," he confided. "If you believe in a God who is big enough to solve the problems of humanity and provide the strength to be triumphant, you preach it and leave the rest up to God. If you have that kind of faith, God will see to it that you don't fail. If you don't have that kind of faith, you might as well get started in another profession." He confessed to me that he had some serious doubts. "Well," I told him, "I don't know many people who have not entertained some doubts at one time or another in life. You preach your faith and pray about your doubts, and God will see you through." It is our business to proclaim the faith, not talk about our doubts. Bishop Authur J. Moore wrote: "We sing a song at midnight, not because of the darkness, but because we are sure the morning will appear."

I have discovered, in the course of counseling, that we must constantly remind ourselves of four major truths concerning the Christian faith. They are truths that Jesus taught, and by which He lived His own life. They are like lanterns guiding us safely through the dark nights of life:

(1) Reconcilation between God and man is possible. Two churchmen were discussing the unsearchable riches of Christ, and one said to the other, "Tell me, what is the best news you know about God?" His companion replied, "He forgives my sins."

I'll have to confess that I do not fully understand how God can forgive us our ugly sins. However, I am fully convinced that everywhere in the life, death, and the resurrection of our Lord we see evidence of God's unfathomable love, which is behind His forgiveness. The sins of our lives repudiate this divine love. In spite of this fact, God continues to love us and is willing to forgive us.

Suppose Jesus had said to the woman at the well, when she freely admitted that He knew even the secrets of her heart, "You are just a poor, sinful woman whose deeds are so evil and whose soul is so stained that you are beyond redemption." He didn't say that. Instead, He told her of the water that would last her an eternity. When Jesus revealed Himself unto her, she hurried back to the city, leaving her water jug, to tell others that she had seen the Christ. Her life must have been transformed, because many of the Samaritans believed because of her testimony. Others believed because they, too, heard Jesus speak.

Suppose Jesus had said to Peter, when he denied Him, "You have had your chance. I cannot forgive you." Jesus did not say that. Instead, He recommissioned Simon Peter to do His work. Jesus said to Peter, "Feed my lambs. . . . Feed my sheep" (JOHN 21:15-16).

When Jesus heard the sincere cry of the thief who was dying beside Him on another cross, He did not say, "You must pay for your crimes." The thief admitted his ugly sins; he said, ". . . we receive the due reward of our deeds . . ." (LUKE 23:41). When he said to Jesus, "Lord, remember me when thou comest into thy kingdom," Jesus replied, ". . . To day shalt thou be with me in paradise" (LUKE 23:42-43).

You see, God forgives us even when we do not deserve it. I suppose, if the truth were fully known, we never deserve His forgiveness. Dr. E. Stanley Jones once told of a government official in India whose job took him away from home weeks at a time. He was greatly tempted and soon fell into the ways of shame and dishonesty. His wife was a devoted Christian, and the man's sins continued to haunt him, so one day he decided to tell his wife the whole wretched truth. He called his wife into his room and told her the sordid story. It came as such a shock that she fell against the wall and stood there with tears streaming down her face. She looked as though she had been struck with a whip, and her face turned pale as death as the meaning of his words began to dawn on her. Later he said, "In that moment, I saw the meaning of the cross. I saw love crucified by sin." When it was all over, she told him that she still loved him and would not leave him, but would help him back to God and a new life. That is what God has been saying across the centuries. God says, "I won't leave you; I'll help you back to life if you'll just give Me your hand."

I like to read the want ads. Recently, I saw a little two-line ad that really intrigued me. It read: "Dear Carolyn: Come back home. We can patch things up. I love you. Chuck." I wonder why Carolyn left home! Perhaps it was because of Chuck. But then, it could have been because of her own wrongs. Actually, it doesn't matter why she went away. The only thing that matters now is that Chuck loves her and things can be patched up. God has been telling us that for centuries. It does not matter what sins cause us to be away. God keeps saying, "Come on home. Things can be patched up. I love you. God."

(2) Don't be afraid of life. Fear paralyzes us. It robs us of our effectiveness. Faith and confidence give us strength. All through the Bible, we are told to trust God. He keeps us from being afraid. After the death of Moses, Joshua was chosen by the Lord to lead Israel. Of course, the task was too big for mere human

strength. God frequently gives us opportunities that we could never achieve alone; we must have His strength. Listen to the word of the Lord, speaking to Joshua: "Be strong and of a good courage; be not afraid, neither be thou dismayed: for the Lord thy God is with thee whithersoever thou goest" (JOSHUA 1:9).

The Lord was saying some very significant things to Joshua: (1) He was urging him to remember his own abilities and strength; (2) He was stressing the importance of faith—"Keep your courage high"; (3) He was reminding Joshua to guard against fear and dismay, telling him never to look at a task and say, "I will fail," even before he began; (4) the Lord was assuring Joshua that He would go with him every step of the journey. Victory is assured, when we know God is with us. What more do we need than to hear God say, "I will be with thee: I will not fail thee, nor forsake thee" (JOSHUA 1:5)?

Remember that thrilling story about a very important man who ran to find Jesus? His name was Jairus. His little daughter was critically ill and he was making a desperate attempt to save the one who was close to him. When he told Jesus about his problem, Jesus knew how much the little girl meant to her father, and He agreed to go and help. While they were on the way to the home of Jairus, a servant came and said to Jairus, "Thy daughter is dead: why troublest thou the Master any further?" Jesus heard the report and turned to Jairus and said, "Be not afraid, only believe" (Mark 5:35-36). As long as we live in the presence of God, we need not be afraid.

While preaching in another state, I was asked to visit a saintly lady who was critically ill. I didn't look forward to the visit, but after it was all over, I was mighty glad I saw her. It was not difficult to see that her life was ebbing away. Yet on her face was a radiance that expressed her faith in God. I am sure she was an inspiration to all who knew her. She was not afraid to talk about death. For her, it was merely changing her place of residence. Like Paul, she believed that ". . . the sufferings of this present time are not worthy to be compared with the glory which shall be revealed in us" (ROMANS 8:18). She said "I have spent the past

fifty years walking with God and I am not afraid of tomorrow."
When we walk with God as that woman walked with Him, we
shall find the inner strength to face each tomorrow without
fear.

God does not send us into unknown lands; rather, He invites us
to follow Him. You may be certain that no matter how steep and
rugged the hill, or how deep and black the chasm, or how big and
heavy the burden, if you are sensitive to God you can see His
footprints and feel the touch of His hand. When you walk
through some dark valley, remember Gethsemane; and when the
weight of the world is upon you, remember Calvary.

(3) God never fails us. In one of the great affirmations of faith,
we read that God's Will "is ever directed to His children's good."
We also believe that in God we can find an adequate supply of
"strength and help in time of need." That is to say, God's grace is
adequate for man's every need. Not only is it adequate, but it is
also available to the last and the least.

I often say to people, "You may not get what you want out of
life, but if you will accept it, God will give you what you need."
The one thing we ought always to remember is that we may not
always get our way, but we always have God.

I think of St. Paul as a spiritual giant. Yet he knew the hard
realities of life. He was shipwrecked, beaten, ridiculed, and cast
into prison for his faith. He also suffered from a physical handi-
cap. He referred to it as a "thorn in the flesh."

In spite of the persecutions Paul endured, he was able to say, "I
can do all things through Christ which strengtheneth me" (PHIL-
IPPIANS 4:13). Paul did not get the exact answer he wanted from
God when he prayed for the "thorn" to be removed. Nevertheless, he had God, and he discovered that no matter what a person
must bear, if God is with him he can be triumphant.

We do not always know what God said to Jesus in answer to
His many prayers. We have every reason to believe that when
Jesus prayed, He always left the place of prayer, knowing that
God was with Him. Once Jesus prayed, ". . . My God, my God,
why hast thou forsaken me?" (MARK 15:34). Had that been the

last word Jesus uttered on the cross, I would be greatly disturbed. Yet He continued to speak, which was evidence that He felt God's presence. His final word from the cross was one of perfect trust and confidence: "Father, into thy hands I commend my spirit . . ." (LUKE 23:46).

God never promised to make life easy for us. He never promised to keep us free from disappointments and hardship. He did not say, "Don't worry, you won't ever be hurt." The promises are: "My grace is sufficient . . . ," "I will be with thee . . . ," "I will not fail thee."

(4) God created us for eternity. This is God's gift to man. None of us would claim that he has done anything that makes him worthy of an endless life, but this is our claim because it is God's promise.

Many people look with great dread upon death. For the Christian it is merely a second phase of life. The Christian passes through the valley of death with great expectations and holy aspirations. I am convinced that he will not be disappointed.

At our house we have two small boys who are learning the Twenty-third Psalm. I often need to prompt them when they forget the next line. After the phrase, "Yea, though I walk through the valley of the shadow of death, I will fear no evil . . . ," I often have to help them. I simply say, "Why won't you be afraid?" That is all I need to say. They continue, ". . . for thou art with me; thy rod and thy staff they comfort me" (v. 4).

J. Wallace Hamilton reminded us of the famous king who appointed a man to say to him each day, "Philip, remember thou art mortal," lest he forget his kinship with God and eternity.

I have always been fascinated by the story of the prodigal son. I have often wondered about the feelings and thoughts of the father. I have an idea he was very restless every moment his son was away. He must have thought, "I could not keep him from going away because he is a grown man and can choose to live as he pleases."

How did the father know that his son was coming up the path? Do you suppose the father sat by the window, looking down the path? Did he take a chair and sit on the front porch and wait? The Scripture reads, "But when he was yet a great way off, his father saw him, and had compassion, and ran, and fell on his neck, and kissed him" (LUKE 15:20).

How long the young son had been away, we cannot tell. I do not believe the father just sat down and waited. That was not in keeping with the character of God as revealed in Jesus Christ. Maybe the father had said to a servant, "I can't stand it any longer. I am going to look for my son." With that, he walked down the path at the very moment his son approached. Before he traveled very far, he saw his son coming up the path and ran to meet him.

No matter for what reason we approach God, we will always find Him coming down the road to meet us. Perhaps we come to Him in search of forgiveness. If so, He will be looking for us, and will even meet us along the road. When we pass from the lights of the earth through the valley of death, we will not be alone. God will be waiting for us with His lantern of love in the darkest valley of all. Let us try to be worthy of such a God.

7

But What Can I Do About My Problems?

A defeated man walked to the center of the Brooklyn Bridge. An eye-witness reported, "He climbed up a part of the super-structure. He paused! Then he jumped!" A few days later the body was found, identified, and buried. In a dingy apartment, a note was found among the man's personal effects: "Life is hell and I have come to the end of the way. I find no purpose in my existence. There is no alternative."

The man did not need money; he had a small fortune in the bank. He could have worn expensive clothes and lived in an exclusive apartment. He chose to live alone—so much alone that he excluded God from his life. When a man commits his life to God, there is never "an end of the way." We come to the end of the way only when we search in our little bags of intellectual achievement and human frailties for the wisdom and strength to face life.

There is always an alternative. There is my way, and there is God's Way; I must make the choice. My way leads to defeat and frustration. God's Way may bring me through a dark Geth-semane, up the slopes of Calvary, or through a lonely valley, but it never comes to a dead end. His Way will eventually bring me to victory. When I enter tunnels of trouble, I can have the com-fort of God's presence. When I bear my burdens, I can have divine strength. When the way is blurred, He offers His hand to guide me.

Two things keep sending me back to the workbench: namely, God has a purpose for every life, and He has the answer to every problem. It is not always easy to find His purpose; nevertheless, He has a purpose for each of us. Like our Lord, we struggle through Gethsemanes in search of answers to our problems. We may not always find the answers we want, but God has an answer for every problem we face.

Recently I was visiting a lovely lady in a hospital, and she told me about a conversation she had had with her doctor. It went something like this: The doctor placed his hand on hers, looked straight into her eyes, and asked, "How much do you want to live?" "I want to live more than anything in the world," she replied. "I love life," she continued. "Well, you must stop smoking immediately," the doctor replied.

Now, I want to ask you a question: How much do you want to live? If your answer is the same as the answer of the woman, then I would reply, "You must stop trying to live alone, and let God have first place in your life."

One of my favorite stories in the New Testament is the one about the healing of the nobleman's son. In this simple little story, we discover some simple steps that will bring us from hopelessness to hope, and from defeat to victory.

A few days before the incident, Jesus had been in Jerusalem. There, many people heard Him speak and some were healed of their diseases. Then, in Samaria, many believed. Christ's fame was spreading, but the people of Galilee seemed to be indifferent to Him. But when He reached Cana of Galilee, the people received Him gladly. Many of them had been in Jerusalem during the feast and had heard Him speak, and they were impressed with the sensation He caused.

People flocked around Him, hoping He would perform some exciting miracle. Strange rumors about the power of Christ had spread throughout Galilee. They reached a nobleman in Capernaum who walked the floor with a sick son. At such a time, when we have done all we know how to do, and still failure seems evident, we all scan the horizon to see if we can find a glimmer of hope. Suddenly the nobleman thought of Christ. "Someone told me Christ was in Galilee. Yes," he said to himself, "Christ is in Cana. That is not more than twenty-five miles away. I will go to Cana and see if Christ can help me." So he took the first step: (1) let's call it resolution; he made up his mind.

To paraphrase Shakespeare, "Experience teaches us that resolution is the only help in time of need." Resolution may not be all the help available, but we must admit that it is the first step. Resolution is a dream that has not yet come true.

Do you have a problem that needs to be solved? You can be a better husband, wife, son, or daughter. You can be a better neighbor, employee, or employer. You can be a better student. But first you must resolve to be *better*. Some people are just about trapped by evil habits. They can be mastered. There are the evil habits of drinking, cursing, gambling; the sins of gossip and promiscuous sexual activity. They can be conquered. The first step is resolution.

You will notice that the man whose son was at the point of death did more than make a resolution: (2) he followed through. He was a busy man, but he let other things wait. He could have made his resolution and left it there. He could have said to himself, "I will just wait, and perhaps Jesus will come to Capernaum." No. First on his agenda was to find Christ.

All of us face the danger of making noble resolutions and then failing to follow through. A young couple decides, before marriage, that they will attend church together. Then there is the temptation to sleep late on Sunday morning, and soon other activities begin to fill the Lord's day. They made a good resolution, but they failed to follow through. A student may decide, at the beginning of the quarter, to study diligently and to improve his academic record. Suddenly, he finds himself facing final examinations without having followed through on his resolution.

I remember visiting a family almost ten years ago and talking about the church. This family never attended church. The father said, "We know we should be attending church, and we will get started as soon as summer is over and school starts." School began, fall came, and winter's snow glistened on the trees, and still the family had not been to church. Another call brought a similar confession: "We know we should be in church, and we have all agreed to come. We will begin after Christmas." Christmas came, and the flowers of spring waved gently in the breeze, and the family did not come near the church.

The years slipped by, and one day a tearful mother came to the office. "I don't know whether you remember me or not, but you came to see us and invited us to your church. We never came, and perhaps it's too late now. My husband is home drunk and my young son is in the juvenile jail. Will you go visit him?"

I went to see the boy, and when his case came to court the judge asked the young man, "Do you attend church?" The boy stammered and then gave that embarrassing reply, "No, sir, your honor." "Do your parents go to church?" was the next question. A big lump came into the boy's throat, and he dropped his head, "No, sir!" Then the judge looked at the boy's parents and said, "This does not excuse the boy of the crime he has committed, but I don't see how you can expect much more from your son unless you try to teach him and set a good example before him."

George Eliot wrote, "The only failure a man ought to fear is failure in cleaving to the purpose he sees to be best." Just one question: Do you follow through in the purposes you believe to be best in life?

Notice the next step the nobleman took: (3) he asked for help. "Sir, come down ere my child die" (JOHN 4:49). Jesus said, "Go . . . ; thy son liveth" (v. 50). Many people lose their faith if prayer does not always bring the results they want. There are some sweeping promises in the New Testament concerning prayer. They are frequently misunderstood. Jesus said to His disciples, "If ye shall ask anything in my name, I will do it" (JOHN 14:14). This means that you must ask in the Spirit of Christ. It means praying the prayer you believe Christ would pray, if He were in your place.

I received a letter from a woman who had read one of my books: "I prayed, as you suggested, but my prayer was never answered." Then she wrote about losing her husband and how hard the past year had been. This was my answer: "God does not always take our advice when we ask Him to remove some burden or lead us around some storm, but He will give us the strength to bear the load and lead us safely through the storm, if we will ask for His help." This I believe.

The nobleman believed: (4) he was willing to trust Christ. He did not hurry home. He knew within his heart that his little boy would get well. The next day his servants met him and told him his son had had a change for the better. The news came as no surprise, because the man had believed the words of Jesus.

So many of us are afraid to trust God. I remember the story about the woman who boarded the streetcar, carrying a heavy bag in one hand. She paid her fare and held onto her luggage. The conductor said, "You can put your baggage down, lady; the streetcar will carry it for you." That is a parable of life. We have a lot of baggage that ought to be committed to God through prayer. Let us not carry these cares, worries, and fears around with us. Let us give them to God and He will carry them for us.

We are actors in the drama of life. The Author chooses the parts we should play. The Greek philosopher Epictetus reminded us: "If it be His pleasure that you should act a poor man, see that you act it well; or a cripple, or a ruler, or a private citizen. For this is your business: to act well the given part; but, to choose it belongs to Another."

Dr. Samuel Shoemaker tells the delightful story of an elderly woman who was knocked down by a tire that flew off a passing truck. The accident left her with a broken hip and confined her to a small room for the rest of her days. There is always the chance that one will grow bitter, or at least become impatient with such circumstances. Not that lovely lady! When Dr. Shoemaker stood by her in the hospital, she looked up from her bed of intense pain and, with a wonderful smile, said, "Well, I wonder what God has for me to do here." Is our faith in God that strong? Do we believe that, regardless of the circumstances that surround us, God has something for us to do? Such a wholesome attitude toward life will keep us from growing sour or denouncing the wisdom of God and doubting His love.

The belief that God will keep His promises to us will relieve us of loads of anxiety. To believe otherwise buries us under a mountain of futility and hopelessness.

"But what can I do?" you ask. You can resolve to be better. You can follow through on your resolutions. You can ask God to help you. You can, by the grace of God, trust Him.

8

Five Steps to a Better Life

There is a gripping scene in Harry Wilson's book *The Seeker,* where young Bernal comes to his grandfather to inform him that he has decided not to enter the ministry, and cannot accept the traditional views of God that his grandfather preaches. After a lengthy discussion, the old man looks into the face of his grandson and says, "I have no claim upon you; and I shall be glad to provide for you—to educate you further for any profession—away from here—from this house."

They were stinging words. Bernal did not expect them from his granddad. "Thank you, sir," he replies. "I could hardly take anything further. But I will go . . . I will take a small sum to go with—enough to get me away. . . ." Slowly, the boy turns and walks away. The old man falls on his knees and prays for Bernal. His sobs choke and shake his body.

At early twilight, Bernal comes to say goodbye to his grandfather. He makes his way to the study door for a final word: "I believe there is no One above Whose forgiveness I need, sir—but I shall always be grieved if I can't have yours. I do need that." The old man stands by the open door. "You have it," he says. "I forgive you any hurt you have done me. . . . For that Other forgiveness, which you will one day know is more than mine—I—I shall always pray for that."

As Bernal walks slowly out the door and across the lawn, Nancy calls to him. They talk for a while, and finally Nancy asks a burning question: "What are you, Bernal?" "Nothing, Nance—that's the trouble," he replies. "But, where are you going, and what for?" she continues. "I don't know either answer . . . ," he retorts.

It is not enough to know many fascinating theories about God. One may know the doctrines of the church and the latest twist in theological thinking, but unless he comes face to face with God, and commits his soul to the keeping of the Great Shepherd of the sheep, he will feel the emptiness of soul that Bernal's answer reflected when Nancy asked, "What are you?"

We know God did not make us to be a "nothing." He made us to be noble and to live on life's highest plateaus, where the breeze can be heard through the tall pines like the song of a mockingbird. Little wonder that Bernal didn't know where he was going and for what. The purpose of life is always blurred when one is not committed to a purpose beyond his own selfish desires.

If we are to find the purpose of life, we must look beyond selfish ambitions, which, after our goals have been attained, bring only pleasure to ourselves. Material things have a way of blurring our vision and blinding us to the sunlit peaks of spiritual achievement. A man must look at the stars and listen for the whispers of God before he discovers that his life counts; before he sees, on the distant horizon, an eternal purpose for his existence.

A man called and wanted to know if I would see his son. "If your son wants to see me, I'll be glad to talk with him," I replied. "He'll see you," the father responded. The appointment was made and the young man came. I believe in direct counseling, so I began by saying, "Your dad tells me that you are a little confused about the purpose of life!" "That's right, sir," he said, "but I believe my dad is a little mixed up, too." "Tell me," I asked, "what do you want out of life?" "What I want out of life," he answered, "could be summed up in one word—money."

The young man is not unlike a lot of other people I know. I haven't met a man in my life who wouldn't like to make a million dollars, and I know some people who have already reached the million mark and they want to make more.

"Son, I pity you. Even if you make ten million dollars, you will be, of all creatures, most miserable. Money can buy luxurious mansions, flashy sports cars, fine clothes, and adventure, but these will never satisfy the deepest longings of the soul. You know the things that money can buy, but let me tell you some of the things money cannot buy. The richest man in the world cannot buy health, love, and happiness. I don't care how much money you have, you cannot buy courage, forgiveness, and the inner peace that comes when one is sure that all is well with his soul. These are the things that make this journey through life worthwhile."

There was a long pause and I could tell, by the look on his face, that the young man was giving some consideration to what I was saying. "I'd never thought of it that way," he answered. "Maybe I have been wrong," he continued; "I'll think about what you've said."

"There isn't anything evil about money," I told him. "The evil slips in at three points: how you make it; why you make it; and how you spend it. Lift your sights until you see something greater than just making money, and move in that direction." He thanked me and left.

How can we make life better? Did you ever give any serious thought to that question? If General Motors didn't give some serious thought to the question of how to make better automobiles, it wouldn't be long before they could hang a sign on their factories which read, GONE OUT OF BUSINESS.

I want to suggest five steps that you and I can take in making life better, not only for ourselves, but for those around us:

(1) Be cheerful. Jesus said, ". . . be of good cheer . . ." (JOHN 16:33). It isn't easy to be cheerful all the time, but most of us could be cheerful more often than we are if we worked at it a little harder. No one likes to be around a gloomy person. An old grouch who sees the world through glasses of pessimism won't be bothered with friends dropping by to see him all through the day.

While visiting a lady who had been on a sickbed for more than fifteen years, I was amazed at her cheerful spirit. She had no hope of ever taking a walk among the flowers and trees she loved so much. Poor health sentenced her to that bed until death released her. Yet there was a cheerful smile on her face as I entered the room. She talked about the beautiful flowers in a vase on the little table by the bed. She expressed her gratitude for the green leaves that waved in the breeze outside her window. She spoke freely about her many friends and the goodness of God. When I complimented her on her cheerfulness, she replied, "I decided two things a long time ago. First, complaining will neither help me nor those who pass this way. Then, since this is the workbench where life has placed me, I want to show those who come this way that God provides the power to walk triumphantly through the dark valleys of life."

Jesus, more than anyone else, knew the hard realities of life. He felt the sting of disappointment in those in whom He had placed His trust. He knew what it was like to be hurt by those closest to Him, and He experienced the pain of the leather whip on His back, the bits of jagged metal tearing His flesh. Yet our Lord said, ". . . be of good cheer . . ." (JOHN 16:33).

A governor of one of our states tells the story of a patrolman who had a grand sense of humor. The governor was always glad to see the patrolman coming because he knew he would have a funny story to relate. After dealing with the perplexing and pressing problems of the state, the governor was able to relax in the presence of a cheerful person. To be able to see the cheerful side of life, and to pass it on, is a ministry that will help lighten burdens and release the pressures of our tense world.

(2) Encourage the people you meet on the path of life. History is filled with thrilling stories of those who were ready to give up on some problem, only to be encouraged by a friend and then moved on to victory.

Thomas Edison invented the phonograph, but the first phonograph didn't sound like stereo. Its high tones were harsh and its low tones were muffled. Edison employed a man to correct the situation. The man worked diligently for two years on that one problem and, after so many fruitless experiments, he became discouraged. One day he approached the great inventor and said, "Mr. Edison, I have spent thousands of your dollars and two years of my life, and have accomplished nothing. Surely, if there were a solution to this problem, I would have found it by now. I wish to resign." Edison paused for a few minutes, looked the man straight in the eye, and said, "George, I believe that for every problem God has given us, He has a solution. We may not find it, but someday someone will. Go back and try a little while longer."

It's easy to become discouraged when you meet failure at almost every bend of the road. No man ever climbs to the peak of success who gives up in despair. Edison was a man of tremendous patience, perseverance, and faith. It is difficult to defeat such a combination. When you are about ready to give up on some problem, remember "that for every problem God has given us, He has a solution. . . . Go back and try a little while longer."

When Daniel Webster was a lad of only fourteen, he was enrolled in the Academy at Exeter, New Hampshire. He did well in all his work except declamation. Each student was required to speak twice each month, and young Daniel was timid. He was horrified at the very thought of standing before his fellow students to speak. He studied his speech and committed it to memory, but when he mounted the platform his mind went blank and he could not recall a word of it. It was a moment of great embarrassment as he stood speechless on the stage. He made a second attempt and failed. Suppose no one had offered a word of encouragement to Webster. He would have finished his studies and probably would have gone back to New Hampshire to work on his father's farm. But his principal encouraged and helped Webster over his speaking difficulty. Because someone encouraged him, Webster went on to serve his country admirably and was acclaimed one of the greatest orators of his day.

Jesus was forever encouraging and challenging people to a better life. You, too, can offer a word of encouragement to those who walk beside you down the road of life. You'll be better for it, and the world will be better too.

(3) Remember that a little word of kindness can change a life. Phillips Brooks said, "If there is any good that I can do, or any kindness that I can show, let me do it quickly, for I shall not pass this way again." Today is the time to be kind to those around us;

tomorrow may be too late. A little more kindness in some instances could change a cold business office, with its constant clink of machines, into a warm and friendly place to work. Kindness can transform a tense home into a beautiful place where laughter is heard and love lives. Kindness has a way of bringing the best out in us.

Once a little boy who had caused his mother great pain and disappointment because of his naughtiness was changed almost overnight. All of a sudden he was thoughtful and kind. He didn't talk back to his mother any more, and when she asked him to do something, he did it with a smile. Instead of a source of trouble, he became a source of joy. The lad's mother asked, "What has happened to you, John? You have changed so completely!" "Well," John answered, "the other Sunday, as I left church, the preacher put his hand on my head, and said, 'You are a fine lad.' I knew he would be greatly disappointed if he found out that I wasn't a fine boy, so I decided to be as good as possible."

Kindness is a mighty important stone in the foundation of marriage. I was talking to a friend who told me about an incident in his own life. He was a successful businessman, and most of the time he was absorbed in his work. His wife, in addition to the responsibilities of the house, had offered some of her time to worthwhile civic projects. "Suddenly we found ourselves growing apart," he said. "She had her interests and I had mine, and they were taking us in different directions. I was giving too much time to my work and not enough of myself to the family. I got up early and came home late. Then, one day, while sitting at my desk, I began to take inventory of the things that were really important to me. I wrote the names of my children and wife at the head of the list. I realized that they had been pushed out of first place by my work and other things, so I left the office early that day and went by the florist and bought the loveliest bouquet of roses you have ever seen and took them home. You know what my wife said?" he continued. "She said, 'I didn't know you cared any more.' Ever since that day, I've tried to remember that the most important thing in my life is my family, and I can tell you that we've been happy ever since." Kindness is the one ingredient that stirs within each of us the desire to become the best possible person.

Paul wrote, ". . . be ye kind one to another . . ." (EPHESIANS 4:32). Kindness doesn't cost anything, and all of us have the capacity to be kind. There is an old proverb which reminds us that "One can pay back the loan of gold, but one dies forever in debt to those who are kind."

(4) If you want to make life better for yourself and those around you, live your faith. Faith is the basic stone in the foundation upon which progress is achieved. You see, men never accomplish that which they believe is beyond their reach. Columbus discovered the New World because of his faith. Cyrus Field labored thirteen years in preparation to bring the Old World alongside the New. He believed a cable could be placed on the floor of the ocean and speed communications between Europe and America. Two failures were enough to cause every member of the syndicate, except one, to advise Mr. Field to abandon the project. His faith and perseverance were rewarded; the cable was triumphantly laid and communications were established between the two continents.

Faith climbs mountains that doubt can never ascend. Faith will bridge chasms that doubt could never cross. Christian faith keeps us going, no matter how dark the night or how heavy the burden. Do you remember those thrilling words of Tennyson:

> . . . cling to faith. . . .
> She sees the best that glimmers thro' the worst
> She feels the sun is hid but for a night,
> She spies the summer thro' the winter bud,
> She tastes the fruit before the blossom falls,
> She hears the lark within the songless egg,
> She finds the fountain where they wail'd "Mirage!"
>
> "Faith"

A young college student, whose cynicism seemed to be his most distinguishing characteristic, almost lost his grip on life. Like a flash in the night, he thought of his old professor of religion, in whose class he had sat for a quarter. The professor had lost a son during World War II. Later he watched his wife suffer for months with an incurable disease. Then he suffered a heart attack, and for four weeks lay flat on his back. Yet, through all of it, he had an unwavering faith in God.

The student, in his desperation, turned to the professor. "I guess I haven't found the meaning and purpose of life," he confessed. "Do you know God?" the professor asked. "I have never believed in a personal God," the student replied, "but I'll believe in God because you believe in Him." I dare say the professor had never received such a glorious compliment in all his life! All of us know that it is not sufficient to believe in God because someone else believes in Him, but it is a good place to start. We must believe in God because of what He does for us. The question I want to ask is this: Would anybody believe in God because of your faith?

Jesus didn't shrink from the cross. He prayed that God would provide some other way, but He also prayed, ". . . thy will be done" (MATTHEW 26:42). That is the essence of faith. Jesus was saying, "Father, I'll trust You. If I am placed upon a cross, I know the cross is Your will and is best for humanity." That is the kind of faith that always triumphs.

(5) Finally, life is better when we forgive those who hurt us and find God's forgiveness for our own sins. Forgiveness is a divine quality that heals our broken relationships. It makes us feel clean on the inside.

Jesus didn't come to coddle the rich, pamper the intellectual, or humor the upper crust of society. He made His mission unmistakably clear: He came to seek and to save the lost, and to redeem humanity.

Take a look at that enthralling scene recorded in Luke. The disciples had been fishing for a long time without success. Jesus asked Peter to launch out into the deep and let down the nets.

Peter responded only because it was a request from the Master. He didn't expect to catch any fish, and when the nets were lowered, they caught so many fish that help was summoned to bring them to shore. Then Peter fell down before Jesus, and said, "Depart from me; for I am a sinful man, O Lord" (LUKE 5:8).

Two things were evident to Peter. He discovered, in that moment, the unsearchable riches of Christ and the spiritual poverty of his own soul. He knew that he was dependent upon the mercy of God and needed forgiveness.

Simon Peter was not always Saint Peter. The writer of the Gospel did not try to conceal his stumbling footsteps. He was impatient, crude, and often egotistical. He made many blunders, but we find it easy to forgive Peter because of his unwavering faithfulness and perseverance. His life didn't end with a blunder. When Peter came to the end of his earthly journey, flags of victory were flying and bugles of triumph were blowing.

After the crucifixion, the mourning women came to the tomb early in the morning on the first day of the week. Do you remember the message our Lord left with the one standing guard? ". . . go and tell his disciples, and Peter, that he will be in Galilee. . . . You will see him there . . ." (MARK 16:7, PHILLIPS).

Simon Peter must have been brooding. He had failed his Master; he had denied Him at a crucial point. Could he ever feel clean again? Even if the Master were alive, could Peter ever look Him in the face? Perhaps he thought of the words of Jesus: "No man, having put his hand to the plow, and looking back, is fit for the kingdom of God" (LUKE 9:62). That message, ". . . tell his disciples, and Peter . . . ," must have been like a drink of fresh water to a man whose throat was parched and whose lips were cracked. Peter hung onto every word that fell from the lips of the messenger. "Did He really call my name?" Peter listened again as the messenger repeated those words. Peter must have said to himself, "He still wants me! Even after what I did the night of the trial and the day of the crucifixion? That means He still believes in me, and I'll have a place to work for Him."

Can't you just see Peter on that dusty trail as the disciples tramped toward the Sea of Galilee? He walks ahead of the group, his heart beating with an exultant joy. Now there is hope in his heart where there was once failure and shame. The past is stained with ugly deeds, but the future is full of hope! Peter is on his way to see Jesus, and that makes the difference.

Now, when we come face to face with ourselves, and see the ugly deeds of our lives, and feel the hopelessness that Peter felt let us listen for that message that comes from the Master. He will meet us and forgive us and put the stars back in our lives. The Master gave Peter another chance. He gave the adulterous woman another chance. He'll give us another chance if we will come to Him. He will not turn us away.

Not only do we need God's forgiveness, but we need to forgive each other. There is a thrilling story in Ian Maclaren's book *Beside the Bonnie Brier Bush* which illustrates this fact. The young minister John Carmichael and Lachlan Campbell, one of the leading members of John's church, had engaged in some unpleasant words over some of the things that had been said from the pulpit. After prayer and some discussion about the problem with a saintly member of his congregation, the young minister decided to visit Lachlan.

As the young minister approached, Lachlan was busy binding up the wound of a lamb that had lost its way and hurt itself. When the wound was thoroughly cleaned and bound up, Lachlan stood and looked into Carmichael's face and held out both his hands to greet him.

The young minister spoke first. "You and I, Lachlan, have not seen eye to eye about some things, lately, and I am not here to argue which is nearer the truth. . . . But once I spoke rudely to you, and often I have spoken unwisely in my sermons. You are an old man and I am a young man, and I ask you to forgive me and to pray that both of us may be kept near the heart of our Lord, Whom we love and Who loves us."

Campbell replied, "You have done a beautiful deed this day, Mister Carmichael; and the Grace of God must have been exceeding abundant in your heart. It is this man that asks your forgiveness, for I was full of pride, and did not speak to you as an old man should; but God is my Witness that I would have plucked out my right eye for your sake." They knelt down together and prayed.

No matter what our station in life is, we need God's forgiveness and we need to forgive one another. This is not an easy step to take, but it'll make our lives, as well as those around us, better.

9

How to Get Rid of Self-Pity

The world is full of sick people. The No. 1 disease in this country is one I choose to call selfishness. It is easy to become intrigued with the self. Those who have will admit that it is a one-way street.

The symptoms of selfishness are discontentment and unhappiness. Our world becomes so little that God's purpose cannot be seen. We lose sight of the horizons that challenge us. The call of adventure slowly fades into the distant hills. The horizons that challenge are still there, and the echo of adventure still calls, but we can neither see nor hear. We have become infected with ourselves.

The most miserable people in the world are those who feel only their hurts, and remember only their disappointments, and are interested only in their own victories. I don't always agree with Bertrand Russell, but he speaks to this point with an amazing insight into human nature. "Nothing is so dull," he wrote, "as to be encased in self, nothing so exhilarating as to have attention and energy directed outward."

The most difficult mountain to climb is the mountain of selfishness. The person who conquers himself stands ready to serve a needy world. Louisa May Alcott wrote a little verse called "My Kingdom":

> I do not ask for any crown
> > But that which all may win;
> Nor try to conquer any world
> > Except the one within.
> Be thou my guide until I find,
> > Led by a tender hand,
> The happy kingdom in myself
> > And dare to take command.

The road to selfishness will eventually bring us to the house of self-pity. Here we lament the misery in our hearts. In such a condition we often get the feeling that no one really cares about us and the world has been unfair to us. We pull the shades, close the doors, turn out the lights, and curse the darkness. One would think that here was a place from which there was no return.

I keep saying to people who bear heavy burdens, experience deep sorrow, and face anxiety that no situation is ever hopeless. God will never give us a task that is impossible to achieve if we are faithful to Him. Jesus said, ". . . for with God all things are possible" (MARK 10:27).

Let me make some practical suggestions that will help us to move out of the house of self-pity and away from the road of selfishness toward a life of happiness and service:

(1) Take a look around. If you feel that all the trouble of the world has settled in your backyard, it won't take you long to see the folly of such a belief. Even the casual observer will be able to see the bleeding sores of a staggering humanity. Jesus warned, "In the world ye shall have tribulation . . ." (JOHN 16:33). He never suggested that there was even the slightest possibility that you could pass this way without ever feeling the sting of disappointment or the sharp pain of grief. This is a part of the price you must pay for the mountains of joy you know as you pass through life.

If you ever get the idea that God has singled you out and placed the heaviest cross upon you, come by my office and let me share with you some of the morning mail. Linger for a while and listen to the people who come in search of a light of hope. Go with me to the hospitals and visit the rooms in which you can almost hear the flutter of an angel wing.

Any self-pity that you may have will be easily transformed into compassion when you see the troubles others bear. I wish you could have been with me recently when I walked into Room 2219 in Egleston Hospital. In that room was a mother, a father, a grandfather, and a sick little boy. The little patient was not yet six years old. I helped the little fellow put a toy together. He won't get to play with it very much. Before long, he'll be playing around God's great throne.

I wish you could have heard that mother say, "This thing is hard to accept, but with God's help we will accept it. We are mighty thankful that thus far our boy has been able to be up and to play a little each day. This is not what we want, but we know God will give us the strength we need to face it." You couldn't stay there very long before a big lump crawled into your throat. When you left, you wouldn't be thinking of a single problem that was yours. Rather, you would go away saying a prayer for that little boy and his mother, father, and grandfather. You would likely ask God to give them strength, and before you said "Amen," you would probably thank God for some of your own blessings.

If you take the time to look around you, you will also discover that others have been triumphant in spite of their troubles and sorrows. The trials and tribulations of life need not defeat us. When Beethoven lost his hearing, he did not place the tools of life upon the shelf and quit. He went on to write his greatest music, and it will inspire and thrill the souls of men as long as good music is played. Milton was completely blind at the age of forty-five. Yet he continued to write, feeling that blindness was no excuse to hide the talent God had given to him. Pasteur suffered a paralytic stroke at forty-six and was handicapped for the rest of his life. Yet he continued to give himself to his work, and all of us would agree that much of modern medicine rests upon his labors.

Take a look around you at the troubles and handicaps others know and remember that many have been triumphant. With God's help, you can be victorious.

(2) Ask God to help you become the person you were made to be. God did not make any of us to be self-centered and miserable. I am convinced that He wants each one of us to be happy.

My mother and father had five children. They taught us to love and respect one another. They took us to church and prayed with us. More than anything else, they wanted us to be Christian. They believe, and I have a feeling that they are absolutely right, that you cannot be genuinely happy unless you are at peace with God.

I once talked to a couple who were having a hard time on the sea of matrimony. The young woman was a patient and devoted wife. She loved her husband and wanted to save their marriage. "I don't believe that divorce is right," she said, "and I'm willing to do anything to make my marriage succeed." I learned that she had gone the second mile and had often turned the other cheek. The husband was a very selfish person who believed that God made him to occupy a throne and, at the same time, live as he pleased. He was stubborn and full of pride. I don't know whether my counsel helped them or not, because I never heard from them again. I had the feeling that the young wife was doing her best, but the husband didn't seem to think he owed anything to the marriage. The truth is, you can't make much of a marriage unless both are willing to try.

The husband expected his wife to have the meals on time and keep the house in perfect order. I told him he had a double standard: one standard by which he wanted to live, and another by which he expected his wife to live. That is true in many marriages. One good rule to remember is this: Make every effort to become the same kind of a person you expect the one you love to be. That is to say, don't make any demands on others that you are unwilling to make on yourself.

We do not achieve happiness by being served, but by serving. For example, there is a lot more happiness in giving a bouquet of roses than in receiving one. Happiness is like a boomerang; it always grows when we make others happy.

When the cultured, rich man came to Jesus, he asked, "Good Master, what shall I do that I may inherit eternal life?" It was evident that he was a student of the Scripture and a good, moral individual. He didn't commit adultery; he did not steal; he had never committed murder, and had always honored his father and mother. In spite of that, the man was not sure of his salvation and knew that he was not completely happy. He was selfish and greedy. Jesus said, ". . . sell whatsoever thou hast, and give to the poor, and thou shalt have treasure in heaven: and come, take up the cross, and follow me" (MARK 10:17, 21). Would it be a bad interpretation to indicate that Jesus was saying, "If you want eternal salvation and genuine happiness, do something for someone else, and in so doing, you will become the person God expects you to become"?

(3) Let God use you. It may be that God will not always permit us to work where we want to serve, but He has work to be done wherever we find ourselves. You see, we often forget that the stars must have a supporting cast, or else there can be no play.

Several months ago, while speaking in another church, I noticed a woman who was facing the sunset of life. After the sermon, I saw her move slowly toward the pulpit; to walk was a real effort. She gently squeezed my hand and told me how much the sermon had meant to her. Then she said, "I retired a few years ago, and there were so many things I wanted to do in the church. I had dreamed of giving all my time to God and His church. Shortly after my retirement, I was stricken with arthritis. I can't do the things I dreamed about, and there are times I can't even attend." With tears falling from her cheeks, she said, "But I can do something: I can pray." We are never useless tools if we place ourselves at God's disposal.

A preacher once quoted a saintly old woman as saying, "God takes a hand whenever He can find it. Sometimes, He takes a bishop's hand and lays it on a child's head in benediction; then

He takes the hands of a doctor to relieve pain; the hand of a mother to guide her child; and, sometimes, He takes the hand of an old woman like me to comfort a neighbor." No matter where we are, if we will hold up our hands God can use them.

There are times when we get in God's way. Instead of being stepping stones, we are stumbling blocks. We influence others by the way we live.

Once, when a leading businessman was approached by a minister about becoming a member of the church, the businessman said, "It might surprise you, preacher, but three of your leading members have blocked the door for me. You know them at church," he continued, "but I know them in the business world." That was a flimsy excuse, we would all agree. God doesn't measure His expectation of me by what others do. Yet, we must remember that, in some measure, we are responsible for our influence. Paul wrote, "It is good neither to eat flesh, nor to drink wine, nor any thing whereby thy brother stumbleth, or is offended, or is made weak" (ROMANS 14:21).

Let us live in such a way that our lives will be a light for those who walk in the darkness, and strength for those who bear heavy loads, and courage for those who are afraid. A blind Englishman was noted for a lantern he always carried. People often asked, "What use is the lantern to you, since you are blind?" The wise old man replied, "I do not carry it to prevent my stumbling over others, but to keep them from stumbling over me." Herein lies the challenge of the Christian faith we profess. Let us make certain that no one stumbles because the faith we profess and the faith we practice are so different.

(4) Be willing to start. Many of us are like the old man who prayed, "Lord, use me in an advisory capacity." I know a lot of people who would be proud to be generals in the Lord's army, but God needs a host of privates.

A man said to me recently, "I volunteered to do the dirty jobs in the church, and I didn't realize there were so many dirty jobs that folks don't like to do." The Lord needs some privates who are willing to say, "Send me down to the front lines where the bloody battles are fought."

This word *readiness* is exceedingly important, and our psychologists have recognized its significance. A child does not talk until he is ready. He doesn't walk until he is ready. You and I must be ready to venture for God before He sends us on a divine mission.

God had a hard time persuading Moses to lead the Hebrews out of Egypt. Before Moses began his difficult mission, he said, "Let me go . . ." (EXODUS 4:18). God calls constantly, but we must respond.

Isaiah had a glorious vision in the temple. God needed a messenger to speak to His people, and suddenly it occurred to Isaiah that he could be that messenger. He responded by saying, "Here am I; send me" (ISAIAH 6:8).

Procrastination is one of Satan's most powerful weapons. If he can persuade one to defer making a decision, he is satisfied. A young couple may be convinced that they should become active in a church. Evil agrees, but it whispers, "Wait until next week." A man convinces himself that his drinking is a problem. It is a problem at work and at home. He tells himself that he ought to quit. Again evil agrees, but it whispers, "Sure, you ought to quit, but wait until next month." A person becomes unfaithful to a marriage vow and is aware of the evil involved. It isn't difficult to convince one that such is wrong. Still evil agrees, but it whispers, "Sure it's wrong, but don't decide today; wait until tomorrow."

You and I do not become spiritual giants overnight. But everyone knows that if we are ever to become the persons God expects us to become, we must take the first step.

An outstanding man, one to whom I have already referred, came to Jesus in quest of the good life. No one had to convince him that to be like Christ was the ideal way to live. He wanted the inner peace that comes to the person who follows Christ, but he was unwilling to make a decision for Christ. Decide, this very moment, that you will make every effort to be the person God created you to be. Keep in mind that you cannot be that person unless you say "Yes" to the claims He has on your life.

I say to a lot of people, "Don't be sorry for yourself; wake up and live." Life may not be all you want it to be, but we can wave the flags of victory if we say "Yes" to God. The circumstances that surround life may not be very pleasant, but the power that can be ours through God is totally adequate.

10

Things I Know About God

The other day a little boy died in a hospital. For several weeks he had suffered from a tumor of the brain. He had the best medical care. In spite of it, he died. Someone asked, "How do you explain something like that?" My reply was, "You don't explain it, but you have to accept it."

Actually, we could make some feeble attempts to offer an explanation. One might say, "It's God's will." I would answer, "Oh, no! I do not believe that!" I cannot reconcile such a death with the Christ who walked the dusty streets of Jericho and the shores of Galilee. I am fully convinced that God wants us to find the answer to such conditions.

Another may say, "This is one of the risks we must assume." All of us know that the privilege of life does not carry with it an immunity from sickness, sorrow, and tragedy. Even this explanation is completely inadequate to assuage our grief and answer the restless questions of the heart.

What are we to do when we fail to find answers to many baffling questions that grow out of our experiences along the road of life? Shall we turn away from God and utterly desert Him because we do not understand all of life? Shall we deny the knowledge of God we do have because we cannot know all about Him? Shall we abandon the faith we have because we do not have all faith?

When reason fails us and logic evades us, we need our faith more than ever. If we trust in God regardless of the circumstances that surround us, He will neither fail nor forsake us. Have you ever thought about the magnanimous faith of Job? How could Job ever have found his way through the tragic events of his life by means of reason and logic? He finally concluded that no human answer to the problems that plagued him would satisfy. Therefore he said, "Though he slay me, yet will I trust in him . . ." (JOB 13:15). He affirmed his faith in God's goodness, and was determined to hold onto it, because faith in God was his only hope.

A friend of mine owns a small plane. When the clouds are low and the fog is thick, he never flies. When the weather is bad, he is quick to tell you there are two good reasons why he wants both feet on the ground: he does not like to take unnecessary chances, and he does not have the instruments to fly in bad weather.

Some months ago, I was flying to New York. The captain spoke to us through the intercom system: "We regret that this part of the trip may be a little unpleasant due to inclement weather. We will be flying through some clouds and may experience a little bumpy flying." Then, with complete confidence, he concluded by saying, "Don't worry, our instruments are working fine and everything is under control."

The big planes continue to fly through the clouds because they have instruments to guide them when the pilots are unable to see where they are going. That is the difference between the man who has a genuine faith in God and the fellow who doesn't. When the storms of life descend upon the person who has no faith, the pressure makes him fall. On the other hand, when trouble comes to the person who really believes in God, he keeps going. His faith keeps him steady.

When Jesus faced Calvary, He couldn't find a logical explanation for the brutal cross. Even though He did not understand the full meaning of it, He knew it must be, and His faith in a God who was both good and wise kept Him from falling. Faith is that quality of a man's soul that compels him to believe and trust God when all the lights of reason have been extinguished.

I know a man who doesn't have a college degree, has never even registered at one of our great universities. If you measure wealth by stocks, bonds, money, and real estate, then he would be listed among the poor. I do not mean that he is poverty-stricken. He owns his own home, has a good job, and drives a nice automobile. If, on the other hand, you measure wealth by character, gentleness, concern for one's fellow man, and love, then this man is one of the richest I know. I could find an army of people who would tell you that his life has greatly influenced theirs. They could list many good deeds that he has done for them and others. I am certain that he has never read a book on theology. He probably wouldn't know who Barth, Tillich, Bultmann, and Kierkegaard are. He couldn't tell you what Brunner thinks about God, but he knows what Jesus thought about God. He could also tell you a great deal about Moses, Joshua, and Jeremiah. He could talk for a long time about Paul, Andrew, and Peter.

There are many things that this man cannot tell you about God, but what he knows about God is worth remembering. The things he cannot explain about God don't cause him to abandon his faith. One might say that he doesn't know much theology, but he knows God. The reason I know so much about this man is that he is my father.

In spite of the fact that a part of God's nature remains concealed, there are some things we know about Him beyond any doubt. Let me suggest some of them:

(1) God comforts us when the walls of sorrow surround us. I often tell people that in all my searching, and in the searching of men of other centuries, no one has found a way around sorrow, but many have found a way through. The psalmist was not exempted from sorrow, but he was fortified with a faith that kept him steady during the trials of life. He said, "Cast thy burden upon the Lord, and he shall sustain thee: he shall never suffer the

righteous to be moved" (PSALM 55:22). He spoke like a man who knew what he was talking about.

Henry Wadsworth Longfellow expressed a keen insight into life when he wrote:

> Be still, sad heart! and cease repining;
> Behind the clouds, the sun's still shining;
> Thy fate is the common fate of all,
> Into each life some rain must fall,
> Some days must be dark and dreary.

"The Rainy Day"

I am not sure that some days *must be* dark and dreary, but I am certain that some *are*.

When sorrow comes, you can find genuine comfort only in God. Sir Harry Lauder, the great Scottish comedian, upon receiving the news that his son had been killed during World War I, remarked: "In a time like this there are three courses open to a man. He may give up in despair, sour upon the world and become a grouch. He may endeavor to drown his sorrow in drink or by a life of waywardness and wickedness. Or, he may turn to God."

The best-known psalm in the Bible is the Twenty-third. Unnumbered millions have committed it to memory. The psalmist admits that he does not know of a detour around sorrow, but he expresses his faith in God's goodness: "Yea, though I walk through the valley of the shadow of death, I will fear no evil: for thou art with me; thy rod and thy staff they comfort me" (v. 4).

I know a man who watched his wife slowly die. He was very much afraid that he could not endure the grief that would come when she died. I tried to assure him that God would not ask him to bear a burden that he was incapable of bearing. After his wife died, the man said, "I realize that before her death I did not have the strength to bear such a heavy cross, but God gave me the strength I needed." The psalmist said, "I laid me down and slept; I awaked; for the Lord sustained me" (PSALM 3:5). We have the assurance that, in all of life, God will supply the comfort we need to meet the sorrows of life. That should not surprise us. Jesus said, "Blessed are they that mourn: for they shall be comforted" (MATTHEW 5:4).

As a minister, I have been privileged to walk with many people through some mighty dark valleys. Most of them have walked triumphantly. A few of them have been defeated by a heavy blow of grief. Those who walked triumphantly accepted divine help and held on to the hand of God. Those who were defeated chose to walk alone and refused to accept God's hand. Jesus said, "I will not leave you comfortless: I will come to you" (JOHN 14:18). He is near when our hearts are broken. His comfort is available, but we must accept it.

(2) God sustains us when our strength fails. Most of us do not travel far down the path of life before we discover that human strength is not enough to cope with our gigantic problems. There may be times in life when we feel that faith in God is not an essential ingredient to successful living. Then there are days when we know that faith in God is imperative. There comes a time when divine strength is the difference between faith and fear, victory and failure.

I remember reading about a young man whose boat capsized about three miles from shore. He began the long swim toward the beach with fear in his heart. While still several hundred feet from shore, he became exhausted. "I prayed," he said. "I don't think I have ever prayed so hard. I told God that either He must take over or I was going under. God took over and I made it to the beach." There are times in every life when either God must take over or a man will go under.

I wonder if Jesus ever prayed for additional strength. Do you suppose He prayed only for insight? He felt the need of constant communion with God as He faced the major decisions of His life.

Go back for a moment and stand in the shadows of Gethsemane

and listen to the words of the Master. Who can understand the agony of His heart? "Father, if thou be willing, remove this cup from me . . ." (LUKE 22:42). What a terrible hour to be deserted by His closest friends! They could have supported Him by remaining with Him. Instead, they all went to sleep. Jesus was well fortified after His experience of prayer. Anyone could look in His eyes and see that He was ready.

After Jesus prayed, the Bible tells us, ". . . there appeared an angel unto him from heaven, strengthening him" (LUKE 22:43). In every trial and during each storm, we can, through sincere prayer, find divine strength.

There is a quotation in which an old Rabbi asks, "What is the worst thing the evil urge can achieve?" and he answers, "To make man forget that he is the son of a King." When your strength fails and human resources fade, don't forget that you are the child of a King, and His riches and resources can be yours.

(3) God loves us with a love that is unfathomable. There may be many unrevealed characteristics about God's nature, but surely humanity cannot misinterpret the many expressions that reflect His love. How else can we explain the incarnation, except to say that it was a message of love wrapped up in the person of Jesus Christ? "We do not deserve such love," you say. You are quite right. Divine love can never be merited; it is always a gift from God.

I once asked our two small sons to tell me why they loved me. Immediately, they began to list the many things that normal parents provide for their children. "You buy our food, clothes, and almost anything we want," they replied. "You buy us candy and toys," they continued. Then I asked them another question: "Did you ever stop to think why I love you so much?" For a moment they were silent. "I'll tell you why I love you so much," I responded. "I love you because you are my sons. I love you because I cannot help it."

Perhaps we have some good reasons why we love God. His gifts are more than we deserve. Did you ever stop to wonder why God loves us? He loves us because we are His sons and daughters. He loves us because it is His nature to love us. Charles H. Gabriel, the writer of the great hymn "My Saviour's Love," wrote about the wonderful and marvelous love of God:

> I stand amazed in the presence
>   Of Jesus the Nazarene,
> And wonder how He could love me,
>   A sinner, condemned, unclean.

We may never know how God is able to love us, but we know that He does.

God's love is indestructible. Robert Southey wrote,

> Love is indestructible,
> Its holy flame forever burneth;
> From heaven it came,
> To heaven returneth.

"The Curse of Kehama"

It is hard to conceive that God's love is greater than the love we have for our children. Yet that is certainly true.

My two sons could do many things that would hurt me deeply and disappoint me beyond description. They could possibly make me ashamed of them; but I am certain that they could never make me stop loving them. God's love is very much like that. You and I do things that hurt and disappoint God. He is not very proud of many of the thoughts we think or the deeds we do, yet we can always be assured of God's love. The man who lives in the gutter and breaks every moral law can still stand up and say, "God loves me." He would be absolutely right.

I'm glad we celebrate Easter each year. While lingering at the cross, we catch a new glimpse of the endurance of divine love. The cross stands as a challenge to each of us. It compels us to give ourselves unreservedly to God. It would be impossible for an observing student of history, or one who is sensitive to the blessings of life, to deny the fact that God loves us. I like J. B. Phillips' translation of the last lines in that great thirteenth chapter of Paul's First Letter to the Corinthians. It reads, "Love knows no limit to its endurance, no end to its trust, no fading of its hope; it can outlast anything. It is, in fact, the one thing that still stands when all else has fallen" (I CORINTHIANS 13:8).

(4) God forgives us when we do not deserve it. Forgiveness is not a beggar's refuge; rather it is the fruit of divine love. Someone has said that the degree to which we are willing to forgive others corresponds to the amount of Christian love in our hearts. When God forgives our sins, He looks beyond all that is ugly and evil about us and claims us as His own.

God has that amazing power to forgive our sins and forget them. The psalmist wrote, "As far as the east is from the west, so far hath he removed our transgressions from us" (PSALM 103:12). God is gracious to forget. "I, even I, am he that blotteth out thy transgressions for mine own sake, and will not remember thy sins" (ISAIAH 43:25).

Once a cleaning woman said to Charles Spurgeon, "I doubt that God will ever forgive my sins. But I tell you, if He ever does forgive me, He will never hear the last of it!" There is a joy that defies description when one has accepted divine forgiveness.

The Good News that God would have us remember is that our sins can be forgiven. Everybody ought to be reminded of this fact each day. No matter how blighted our past may have been, our future can be bright because God stands ready to forgive all our sins. A host of His disobedient children pass by God's throne of mercy each day, and find forgiveness. If our hearts cry out for pardon, we will hear the Master say those thrilling words that He spoke to the woman almost two thousand years ago: "Neither do I condemn thee: go, and sin no more" (JOHN 8:11).

I don't know all I want to know about God, but what I do know is sufficient for this life. What I know about Him, compels me to trust Him to do what is best when the storms of life descend upon me.

11

You Can Be Forgiven

"Can my life be changed?" people frequently ask me. Many people feel the utter despair that covered the soul of the young woman who wrote, "When I look at my past, I am deeply ashamed, and when I get up each morning to face a new day, I tremble with fear." Then she asked the question that a host of people ask at one time or another in life: "Is there any hope?"

God has been lighting candles of hope through centuries of darkness. Micah proclaims, ". . . he will have compassion upon us; he will subdue our iniquities; and thou wilt cast all their sins into the depths of the sea" (MICAH 7:19). Moses said to Israel, "The eternal God is thy refuge, and underneath are the everlasting arms . . . " (DEUTERONOMY 33:27). God is our refuge from the storms of life. He is our refuge when temptations constantly threaten us. He is our redeeming refuge from the sins of life.

God never spoke more clearly concerning our salvation than when the cross was planted on Calvary's hill. The cross is an expression of God's unfathomable love, but equally significant is its magnanimous message of redemption. Here God is revealing to a hostile world that did not understand Christ, and to an undeserving humanity, His plan for divine pardon. There were other ways in which God could have expressed His love for us, but the cross was the only plan He designed to redeem us.

When I write about the need for forgiveness, I know it applies to everyone who reads. Who among us would dare claim that he has lived a perfect life? Our deeds and thoughts would speak out against us. "All we like sheep have gone astray; we have turned every one to his own way . . ." (ISAIAH 53:6). Then, when I write about the possibility of forgiveness, it strikes a responsive chord upon the keyboard of each heart. Paul wrote, "For whosoever shall call upon the name of the Lord shall be saved" (ROMANS 10:13). When I read, "all . . . have gone astray," I am sure it includes me. When I read, ". . . whosoever shall call upon the name of the Lord shall be saved," I am fully convinced that I am also included. You see, no one is ever excluded from God's measureless mercy and complete forgiveness.

Yes, life can be changed. I know a man who at one time was a slave to liquor. It ruined his life, robbed him of his job, and more than once caused him to spend some time in jail. His language was profane and his deeds brought disgrace to himself as well as shame to those who loved him. Then he met the Master, and like Saul who persecuted the Christ, he was changed and became Paul the gallant soldier proclaiming the good he had once despised. Today he lives not merely a respectable life, but a life of honor. His language is no longer vulgar and his deeds bring neither dishonor to himself nor shame to those who love him. When Christ came into his life, he became a new creature. The pages of history are filled with records of those who were locked in dungeons of self-defeat and have emerged triumphantly.

The one hope that remains for humanity is found in God's forgiveness. This is our only means of escaping the consequences of our sins. Bishop Everett W. Palmer, in his book *You Can Have a New Life!* wrote, "Where we need changing, there can be change. A bitter spirit can become sweet with forgiveness and kindness. A sharp tongue can become gentle with love and forbearance. A fear-ridden mind can find the clarity and serenity of faith. A degrading habit can be replaced by noble thought and action. Cowardice can be exchanged for courage; weakness for strength." A miracle can take place in our lives, and our thoughts and actions can be brought into harmony with God's will.

I am one of those who believe that God's forgiveness is of such a magnitude that finite minds will never fully understand it. Perhaps it is just a fact of God's gracious character that we must accept without really knowing how it takes place. We are like the lady who commented, when the mechanic came to repair her automobile, "I just drive the thing; I do not understand how it runs." There are, however, some things that we know about forgiveness:

(1) Forgiveness is largely a divine act. It is the supreme way in which God expresses His love for us. Once, while teaching a membership class of young people, this question was asked of me: "Exactly what takes place during forgiveness?" I tried to explain it. "Forgiveness," I told them, "is a divine act. It is like taking a trip on an airplane. You may pack your bag, make your reservations, purchase your ticket, and even board the plane. You might fasten your seat belt and relax for the trip. That is all you can do. The next move belongs to someone else. The pilot must start the engines and release the brakes before the big plane leaves the ground. Forgiveness is like that. We acknowledge our wrongs and repent of our sins. We come, asking God to forgive. That is all we can do. The next move belongs to God. He never disappoints us. He covers our ugly sins with His divine love. That is forgiveness."

(2) Forgiveness is something we neither earn nor deserve. What could we possibly do that would suggest that we merited forgiveness? We will always be in debt to God because His divine mercy has been extended to our hearts. But we are also indebted to a host of people who lived before us. We are indebted to Isaac Newton, Johann Kepler, and Marie Curie. We are indebted to Beethoven, Benjamin Franklin, and a host of others.

Not too long ago, I found myself sitting at a head table with several people who were being honored. I have never felt more out of place than I did during that event. I can't speak for the dog world, but I felt the way I think a hound dog would feel at a poodle convention. There were several distinguished people; among them my good friend Dr. William R. Cannon, whose outstanding achievements towered above anything I have ever done. When it was my time to speak, I simply said, "I deserve this honor least of any who sit here, but I dare say that no person appreciates it more than I." That is precisely the way I feel when I think of God's forgiveness. I deserve it least, but I am profoundly thankful that He forgives me.

I have more friends than I have earned. I've got friends from Maine to Florida, and from California to Georgia who are better to me than I deserve. A letter came from Florida, from a man who owns a motel. He wrote, "Come and stay as long as you like. It won't cost you a cent." From all over America, I get mail from people who tell me they are remembering me in their prayers. I have said, over and over again, to so many, "I do not deserve your friendship, but I am grateful for it." I feel the same toward God's forgiveness.

(3) Forgiveness is an outright gift from God. I do not agree with George Bernard Shaw that "Forgiveness is a beggar's refuge; we must pay our debts." I just thank God that Shaw was not right.

While walking down the street with me recently, a friend asked me how much I paid for the coat I was wearing. I replied, "It didn't cost me a penny." "Do you mean they are giving them away?" he responded. "The man who brought me this one was giving them away," I answered. You may be certain of one thing: when you see a man whose sins have been forgiven, the clean coat he is wearing is a gift from God. Forgiveness didn't cost him a thing. Actually, it is sin that has the big price tag hanging on it. Sin will cost you inner peace and will separate you from God. It will eventually cost you your soul, unless you repent and accept God's forgiveness.

(4) James S. Stewart wrote: "Forgiveness is not the remission of a penalty; it is the restoration of a relationship." Forgiveness is not so much getting out of paying the price of our sins as it is coming into a right relationship with God.

Perhaps I ought to illustrate the difference between spiritual and physical consequences of our sins. Once God forgives us our sins, we are no longer separated from Him. We can say, with Johann Bengel, "O God, there is nothing between us." There is no longer the burden of guilt or the feeling of estrangement. We are overwhelmed with the feeling that we are at one with God.

On the other hand, one must frequently pay the physical and, sometimes, mental consequences of his sins after he has been forgiven. Take the man who falls into ways of evil living. One day he becomes engaged in a drunken brawl and loses the sight of one eye. While in the hospital, in a critical condition, he realizes the folly of his ways. During the long days of convalescence he spends a lot of time in serious thought, and gives his heart to God. From that time on, he remains faithful to God. In spite of the fact that he has been forgiven his sins, he must pay the physical penalty of his wayward years. Nothing will ever restore the loss of his eye.

The prodigal son was forgiven his sins, and I am certain that his father never mentioned his being away from home. That does not mean that his brother did not remind him of his evil ways. No doubt, the prodigal thought of the days when he was cold and hungry. He must have recounted the days of loneliness and despair. It was not easy for him to readjust to things at home. There is some great consolation in having a right relationship with God, regardless of the consequences we suffer. That was very true with the prodigal. Better to face the consequences of his sins at home where he knew he had the love and understanding of his father. Dr. James S. Stewart, considering this point, wrote, "There might be bitter things to be endured, but what really mattered was that the broken relationship had been restored." Of course, he was thinking about the relationship being restored between the son and father.

I spend a lot of my time offering a word of hope and courage to those who feel that life is no longer worth the struggle. I tell them God can change them. It is sometimes very difficult to scrape away from the flickering lamps of faith the corrosion that is caused by skepticism. Only the power of God can clean those fading lamps again. I am never more keenly aware of the presence of God than when broken relationships are being restored. It is there, more than any place else, that we are dependent upon God.

God's first business is restoring broken relationships. He is trying to make obedient children out of a hostile world. He stands at the door of our hearts, waiting patiently for us to invite Him into our lives. Bishop Arthur J. Moore tells of a lecturer who showed colored slides on religious subjects before the days of motion pictures. One night, the lecturer was in Manchester, England, showing his slides to a great hall crowded with miners and their families. As he flashed Holman Hunt's famous picture "The Light of the World" upon the screen, he stood quietly, because the picture carries its own message. In it, the masterful artist has portrayed the door of the human heart, barred with rusty hinges and nails. Wild grass and brambles cover the threshold. Jesus stands with a lantern in His hand, which represents the light of conscience, and the light on His face glows with assurance and symbolizes the hope of our salvation. He waits patiently because the latch is on the inside of the door.

Suddenly a little girl's voice broke the silence of the hall. "Daddy," she asked, "why don't they let Him in?" "I don't know," her father whispered softly; "you must be quiet." She was silent for a few moments and then, overcome with anxiety, she asked again, "Daddy, why don't they let Him in?" Rather impatiently, the father answered, "Hush! I don't know." Then, as the audience studied the picture, the little girl shouted and all could hear, "Daddy, I know why they don't let Him in. I know why. They must live in the back of the house."

Do you live in the back of the house? If you are lost, you may be certain that it is not God's fault. Calvary is more than you could ask or expect, even from a God whose mercy is everlasting and whose love cannot be measured. Christ stands at the door. He knocks, and waits patiently. Do you hear Him?

Do you have some relationships that need restoration? Some may be filled with resentments and unwarranted prejudice. Others may have a deep sorrow that needs divine healing. Still others may be caught in the grip of some evil habit. Some have the burden of guilt because sins need to be pardoned. Then there are others who need more spiritual strength and fortitude to face the irritating problems of daily living. Whatever your spiritual needs are, they can be met in Jesus Christ. I do not know what your spiritual needs are, but I do know a God who can supply your every need, and who can give you the grace to walk triumphantly through all of life. No life is beyond His help. Jesus said, ". . . for with God all things are possible" (MARK 10:27).

12

When the Lamps of Faith Flicker

A young college student, questioning the Christian faith he had learned as a lad, began to take off what he considered to be the old-fashioned garments of faith and hope. His parents had taught him that God made this marvelous universe, and that apart from God life has no genuine purpose. At the end of the young man's first year in college, he came home to visit his humble parents; he was wearing the garments of skepticism and doubt. He questioned the existence of God.

One day the lad sat with his father under a big oak tree near the woodpile. The old man picked up a piece of soft pine and began whittling. They sat in silence for a while, and finally the boy asked this penetrating question: "Dad, how can we know that God made this universe?" The old man paused for a few minutes and then slowly closed his pocket knife and placed it carefully on the log, along with the piece of wood he had been whittling. Without saying a word, he took his pocket watch out of his pocket and removed the back so the boy could see the many moving parts.

"Son," he began, "look at that watch. There must be more than a hundred little wheels, springs, and gears in that watch. We could carefully take every tiny part out of the case and throw them on the ground, and no matter how many times you repeat that act, those little delicate parts would never accidentally fall into their proper place. Only a master watchmaker could have made that watch in the first place, and only a good watchmaker could make it run again if it stops. Son, all around me I see the footprints of God, and no one could ever convince me that this world just happened. I do not understand all the mysteries of life, but as long as I can see the footprints of God, I know all is well." The saintly old man's faith could see beyond the young man's logic and reason.

Few men stand so far removed from God as to argue with you concerning the existence of some intelligent mind behind this amazing universe. It is rare to find one who will seriously defend the position of an atheist. The evidence in favor of God is so overwhelming that those who are inclined to doubt His existence find little ground to stand upon in the world of reason and intelligence. With one great chorus, and in almost perfect cadence, humanity stands to proclaim our unwavering belief that God is behind the universe. There is too much intelligence and precision in our world for us to be so naïve as to assume that the author of it is mere chance.

Great and humble minds of every century have reverently tipped their hats to a God they did not fully understand, and very often to a God to whom they did not give themselves, but to a God they knew exists. None of the intellectual giants of history have ever claimed to understand God, but most of them have acknowledged His presence and felt His power.

Most of us have little difficulty in believing that God exists and is the Author of the universe. Like men of the past, we acknowledge the footprints of God. Many people with whom I talk are having trouble finding God in the everyday experiences of life. It is not enough to see God's footprints—we must hear His voice and feel the touch of His hand upon us.

We are convinced that God created this universe, but the deep question that cries for an answer in every man's heart is this: "Is God still interested in His creation?" Christianity must be more than a creed. It must reach beyond a set of beliefs that we so glibly say in unison each Sunday.

I talk to people almost every week who find little comfort in knowing that God is behind this creation. If I were to try to comfort some by whispering, "Did you know that God is the Creator of all we see about us?" they might feel like saying, "So what!" People want to know if God is still a part of His creation, or if, perhaps, He has stepped aside to see the show. Does God make up the audience, or is He on the stage of life, prompting those of us who forget our lines and make a miserable mess of the play? Can God be found as we walk across the parched desert, with sand burning our bleeding feet, while lifting the heavy burdens of disappointment and loneliness? Is He near when the human heart is crushed with unexpected sorrow? Is God close by when we sit quietly with our fears and hold in our hands the shattered pieces of what yesterday were noble dreams? Are the words of hope and courage we hear from the pulpit only empty echoes of what the preacher wants to be true? Did Jesus deceive His disciples when He challenged them to stand as true soldiers and promised to be with them in all their struggles? If we can trust the integrity of those giants who have moved across the pages of history, we can conclude that God is inexorably mixed up in the affairs of man. He is near to sustain us when human strength fails, and to guide us when human wisdom deceives us.

Harry Emerson Fosdick wrote, "God outside us is an hypothesis; God inside us is an experience." It is not enough to know about God; we must talk to Him each day and walk through the paths of life with Him if we would be victorious.

Soon after the new clergyman moved into the parish in which Thomas Carlyle lived, he called upon that very wise man. While discussing the needs of the parish, Carlyle said, "What this parish needs, before everything else, is a preacher who knows God other than by hearsay." Well, that is what every church needs, and that is the need of every individual. When a troubled world like ours hears and obeys the voice of God, we will experience much peace, and love will be the motivating force behind our thoughts and deeds.

Men lose their fear when they feel the touch of God's hand upon them. Humanity refuses to give up as long as it feels the power of His presence.

Robert Louis Stevenson felt the touch of God's hand during his long days of illness. During a decisive period in his life, when the light of the future seemed to fade, Stevenson found his way by respondng to the gentle touch of God's hand upon him. "I came about like a well-handled ship," he wrote. "There stood, at the wheel, that unknown Steersman Whom we call God."

The one thing that sends me back to the workbench is not the victories I have known, but the undying belief that God is in life; that if we are sensitive to Him, we will find the grace that forgives our sins, the strength to lift our burdens; that we will feel the touch of the divine hand that will keep us steady during the temptations of life.

I wonder if Breton's beautiful picture "The Song of the Lark" thrills you as it does me. Did you ever notice that there is no lark in the picture? The artist captured the thrill on the face of the peasant girl as she walked toward the field of labor at daybreak. She hears the divine symphonies in the song of a lark amid the common tasks of earth. Flash that picture across the screen of your imagination. Look at the girl. She is on her way to hours of weary labor. Instead of concentrating on the tasks that await her, she hears the song of the lark as it soars through the trackless sky. The melody she hears in this moment will sing in her soul and bless every hour of her toil. You cannot see the lark in this lovely picture, but no one would ever doubt the fact that the peasant girl with the majestic look on her face has heard its thrilling song.

Not too long ago I spent some time with my good friend Henry L. Willet, who is one of America's foremost stained-glass-window artists. As we were driving from my office to his hotel, Henry told me about Bill, who was the vice president of his company. Only a few weeks before, Bill had died suddenly while out of the country on company business. "It fell my duty," Henry Willet said, "to break the sad news to his wife and young son. The day Bill was due back home, we received news of his death." Henry went to Bill's home, and in response to the doorbell Bill's lovely wife came to the door, expecting to find her husband. "Oh, it's you, Mr. Willet," she said, with an obvious look of disappointment on her face. "Yes, it's me," he replied, "and I've got terrible news for you." She interrupted, "It's Bill, isn't it?" "Yes, it is," Mr. Willet responded. "He's dead!" she said, knowing it must be true but waiting for him to confirm it. "I just shook my head, and she knew," Henry told me.

After the terrible shock of that dreadful moment was over, Bill's wife prayed: "O God, thank You for the gracious things You have done to make our life together so wonderful. Give me strength to face these days and to carry on as Bill would want me to if he were here. . . ." She knew God was near and she knew how to find Him. There have been many lonely days and weary nights when all the stars seem to fade from sight, but that young widow has marched with an unfaltering step. "Tell me," I asked, as we rode along the expressway, "what was her secret?" I knew the answer, but I wanted to hear what my friend would say. "Her faith in God was her secret," he replied. "You know," he continued, "as long as a man hangs on to his faith in God, he can face anything life brings him."

After Henry Willet walked away, and on my way back to the office, I got to thinking about what he said: "As long as a man hangs on to his faith in God, he can face anything life brings him." "That's what Jesus was saying to the disciples when they faced an almost impossible situation," I said to myself. Jesus reminded them that "with God all things are possible" (MARK 10:27). That is also the answer Paul received when he prayed for the thorn in the flesh to be removed, "My grace is sufficient for thee . . ." (II CORINTHIANS 12:9). When you and I come face to face with what appears to be the end of the road, let us never forget that "with God all things are possible."

I've lived long enough to know that man must respond to the voice of God if this journey through life is to be meaningful. There are times in almost every life when a man feels that he can get along without God. He plays in gardens of beauty and runs across plains of joy without giving a serious thought to his need of God. In these circumstances, God seems more like a luxury than a necessity. Such moments are exceedingly short in most lives. At other times, God is never considered a luxury but a necessity. When a man climbs over the jagged rocks of temptation and struggles up the steep paths of disappointment, he needs God. When he walks through the deep valleys of sorrow where the lamps of faith flicker, he needs God. When human strength would camp in valleys of defeat and despair, a man must have that divine strength that keeps him marching toward the morning.

Zechariah spoke to a disheartened people. The exiles had returned to a land of ruin, and Zechariah warned them that there was no hope without God. He urged the people to turn back to God, and in Him they would find their true purpose. Zechariah told the people that God had spoken to their fathers, but they would not listen. Now he warned them to listen to God's voice and obey it. "Be ye not as your fathers, unto whom the former prophets have cried, saying, . . . Turn ye now from your evil ways, and from your evil doings: but they did not hear, nor hearken unto me . . ." (ZECHARIAH 1:4).

The exiles wanted to live as they pleased, yet they wanted the peace that comes from knowing God. They were eager to achieve the goal without paying the price. Such thinking prevails today among many of us. Many of us know how we could improve our marriage relationship. Some of our daily acts do not conform to God's will. Some of our young people know how to make their homes happier places to live in, but they aren't willing to do their part. All of us are caught in the grip of some habits that we know we ought to commit to God, and by doing so we would become better husbands, or wives, or sons, or daughters. Yes, God still speaks, but many of us fail to hear Him.

I like what George MacDonald, the Scottish poet and novelist, said more than half a century ago: "You are like little children sitting on the curbstone hunting in the gutter for things. Behind you is a King's palace, finer than Buckingham. In it your Father sits. But you won't listen. You won't even turn around to look. You just keep on hunting in the gutter for things, and it doesn't matter whether it's rotten vegetables, or pennies, or shillings, you find there. They can't make you happy without your Father." God still speaks, but we don't have to listen.

God is still saying what He said to the psalmist: "Be still, and know that I am God . . ." (PSALM 46:10). Waiting very often challenges the very best that is within us. All of us are filled with goals to achieve and destinations to reach. We get irritated when we are hindered by detours or delayed by circumstances. We must be busy meeting appointments and fulfilling the very often ridiculous demands we have made upon ourselves. Most of us have reserved little or no time for waiting.

There are times in life when we are forced to wait. One would find it difficult to imagine the difference we would see in our lives if, at the beginning of each new day, we sat quietly and centered our attention upon God. Our sense of values would change. The tasks to which we give ourselves might be altered. Our working day might be a little shorter. We would be able to face the events of the day with greater confidence and poise.

Sometimes the only thing we can do is wait. If waiting is all we can do, we can be sure that waiting is best. I once read a story about a young lad who had only recently been employed in a coal mine. Soon after entering the dark tunnel, his lamp went out. Fear filled his heart and he hardly knew what to do; the mine was dark, and to move around might bring sudden death. He decided to sit down and wait. Waiting was hard, but it seemed the best thing to do. In the utter dark, every little noise seemed like the thunder of doom. Looking down that dark tunnel, he saw the faint glow of a lamp in the distance and heard a friendly voice say, "Don't be afraid. I've come to get you."

When troubles descend, and you feel there is nothing but darkness around, "Be still," and listen for the voice of God. You can hear Him say, "Don't be afraid. I have come to get you." God waits in the shadows to lead us safely through the dark places when our little lamps go out.

13

Life Is a Million Little Things

Happiness is not an impossible achievement. If you really want to be happy, you can.

A wise man once suggested nine requisites for the person who finds contentment in life: he must have enough health to make work a pleasure; enough money to support his needs; enough strength to battle with the difficulties of life and overcome them; enough grace to confess his sins and forsake them; enough patience to work until some good is achieved; enough charity to help him see some good in his neighbor; enough compassion to move him to help others; enough faith to make real the things of God; enough hope to live above anxious fears concerning the future.

It is impossible to find purpose and meaning in human existence until we relate ourselves to God. It is like trying to tell time by a clock without hands. The prodigal son tried to live without his father; he found only poverty, hunger, and disappointment. I can imagine the prodigal son giving advice to others who were looking for adventure in the far country. "Don't go," he would tell them; "the lights of excitement soon fade, and the fires of adventure turn to cold, gray, and disappointing ashes."

Evil always deceives us. It never satisfies the deep longings of the soul. It may appease us for the moment, but it will never give us the inner peace we need. Evil that brings contentment is like something bought on the installment plan: someday the account must be settled; the consequences of an evil life must be faced. The Bible makes it very clear that our sins will be exposed if they are not forgiven. Life offers every man a choice. He can take what he likes, but he must pay the price.

A man called me one day and asked if I would see him. He insisted that I visit him in his home. I drove out to his house and we sat down in a sparsely furnished room that was in bad need of some major repairs.

"Preacher," he began, "you may not believe my story, but I want to tell you, anyway. I have ruined my life, lost my family, and must face the rest of my days alone. Ten years ago I was making thirty thousand dollars a year. There was laughter in this house, and the furnishings were as fine as money could buy. I sold the furniture and bought whiskey. I beat my wife, and said ugly things to those I love. You are looking at a man who has been defeated by liquor. I am paying for the sins of yesterday." That man could have said, with John Donne, "I count all that part of my life lost which I spent not in communion with God, or in doing good."

I often talk with young couples who are disappointed in marriage. If they begin such a noble adventure with the feeling that it's going to be one long honeymoon, they will become discouraged. There are no moonbeams in a dishpan full of dirty dishes, and there is no stardust on an ironing board loaded with wrinkled clothes. Actually, marriage is composed of a series of little things.

A well-adjusted person is one who is able to cope with the irritating problems of everyday living. Life itself is not one big deed; it is a million little things. It's watching a bird build a nest. It's taking time to pat a little boy on the head. It's looking into the eyes of a pretty little girl. It's walking through the woods on a summer day. It's admiring the lovely clouds as they float overhead. It's going to church. It's discovering the beauty of a sunset. It's finding satisfaction in doing a simple deed for a friend.

You would be unwise to defer this business of living. You may never paint a picture or write a book that will be recorded in history. You may never build a statue or perform some outstanding deed that will assure you of a place in history. But you can leave your mark in a simple and unselfish deed.

History has a way of remembering, with love, those who have lifted the burdens of humanity, brought joy to others, dispersed the clouds of ignorance and superstition, and permitted the light of truth to shine upon man's way. You will never find the names of all the great men and women in our history books. Many great people walk an obscure path.

Greatness is not measured by fame. Elizabeth Taylor is famous, but I dare say she would make no claim to greatness. Cassius Clay is a name known throughout the sports world, and in spite of the fact that he claims greatness for himself, I venture to suggest that he does not measure up.

Greatness is not measured by one's wealth. You may have the ability and opportunity to make money, but along with money comes a responsibility to use it wisely. You do not measure greatness by the size of a bank account.

Greatness is measured by how closely our lives resemble the life of the gentle Galilean. You may be rich or poor, educated or ignorant; you may live in the bright lights of fame or in the shadows of obscurity; but you can never achieve greatness until your thoughts and deeds resemble the thoughts and deeds of Jesus Christ.

There are two primary ways to measure a man. You can measure him on the outside and get his physical dimensions. Then, if you want to determine his spiritual dimensions, you must measure him on the inside. I know a man who isn't over five feet ten inches tall, and he weighs less than 150 pounds. His outside dimensions are average, but on the inside he is well on his way to becoming a spiritual giant.

You are never made great by what you have. Greatness is the result of what you are. What you are is expressed in what you do. Many of us say we believe in God each Sunday. Do we? Do we believe in Him enough to give generously to His work? Do we believe enough to give Him first place in our lives? Is our belief strong enough to stir within us genuine compassion for those who suffer because of poverty, ignorance, and disease?

Recently there was a discussion on television about Dr. Albert Schweitzer and his work in Africa. One man claimed that Schweitzer was an egotist, that he did what he did for himself, and that all his service and sacrifice was an attempt to satisfy his own oversized ego. The other speaker claimed that Dr. Schweitzer's compassion was his motive in giving himself to the dying black men of the jungle. It's strange how we judge the motives of others. If a man keeps everything for himself, we are quick to say that he is selfish. If he denies himself for others, we accuse him of having an oversized ego.

I do not know how God will judge Dr. Schweitzer's work, but I suspect his chances of hearing that "well done, thou good and faithful servant," will be better than that of his critics. He left the comforts of home and moved to the jungles of ignorance, disease, poverty, and suffering where he built fires of healing and lit candles of truth. Did he not go to the "least of these My brethren," to express, not only with the words of his lips but with the deeds of his hands, the Spirit and teachings of Christ? I don't know of another man in this century who has relieved more suffering and lighted more candles of hope in a dark world.

Jesus talked about the importance of simple deeds that grow out of love and concern. He talked about giving a cool drink to the thirsty, sheltering the stranger, feeding the hungry, visiting the sick, and clothing the naked. Whenever we meet a human need with love, we are doing the work of God.

Two men, James and John, with their families, lived as neighbors for many years. They were neighbors in the true sense of the word. One day John's wife became critically sick, and before the crimson colors of the setting sun turned to black shadows, she died. Jim came over to John's house. He didn't have much to say. He didn't know what to say. He put his arm around John's shoulder. They stood for a moment in silence. Jim stayed all night with John. He chopped the wood, kept the water bucket full, and tended the fire. Weeks later, the two men were talking about that long night. "I felt as if I was in the way," Jim said. "You gave me strength," replied John; "I don't think I could have lived through the night, if you had not been there." It was a simple deed, but it was worth doing.

We cannot be Christian in theory only. Christianity cannot be tied up in a neat little bundle of philosophical or theological discussion, no matter how exhilarating it may be. Christianity cannot be confined to the four walls of a lovely sanctuary, or limited to a well-equipped educational building. We cannot restrict Christ to our place of prayer. He must be exemplified by our deeds as well as expressed by our lips.

Roy Angell tells us about an experience that came out of his seminary days. Just before dark, one bitter cold evening, he answered a knock at the small house in which he lived. He found the pastor of a nearby church standing at the door, with flakes of snow covering his coat. Angell invited him in and asked, "What are you doing out in this cold weather?"

There was a glow on the pastor's face as he answered: "I have just seen something that I want to share with somebody. Just outside of town, at the foot of the hill, there lives a little elderly widow. Our church takes care of her. I went to see if she needed anything during this bitter cold weather. As I entered her living room, I saw a little mischief in her eyes as she took me to the kitchen and pointed to a basket of groceries, and a man's coat was draped across the chair. 'You have a man hiding here! Where is he, Auntie? Trot him out.' With a smile on her face, she said, 'You'd be surprised—no, you wouldn't, because you know him. Come to the kitchen window.'"

Near the kitchen window the preacher heard the ring of an ax. After scratching the frost off the window, he saw the president of the seminary chopping wood under the woodshed. Writing later about this incident, Dr. Angell said, "Here was a man with an assignment, a God-given assignment, who had turned aside from his teaching to release some of the Spirit of Christ that so filled his life." The Christ we teach in the classroom and preach in the pulpit must be lived in the street, and in the office, and in the home.

Most of us may never have a chance to do just one big thing in life, but all of us have the opportunity to do a million little things for the King. If we are faithful to the opportunities of each day, we can look back over life when it is over and feel that the journey was worthwhile.

14

All Things Are
Possible With God

Frederick Atkins wrote a book entitled *Standing Up to Life*,
and the title suggests two things: one can stand up to life, and
one can be triumphant. All of us need a faith that sustains. God
did not give us the strength to face life alone, but He did make
it possible for us to find in Him the strength we need.

When I was a lad, we lived about two hundred yards from a
small country store. Frequently, in the evening, my father would
ask me to go to the store for fruit, candy, or something he
wanted. I was afraid of the dark and never looked forward to the
trip. While it was only a short distance, that did not calm my
fears. My father knew I was afraid, and he would always turn the
front light on and frequently walk down to the mailbox and wait
for me. I could look back and realize that I was never out of my
father's sight. I could always hear his voice and see the light
shining on the front of the house.

Life is like that. You and I are never out of sight of the God
who created us. Neither are we out of sight of the lights of the
Father's house, nor the sound of His voice.

The Hebrew poet walked out under the Syrian sky and looked
at the stars and moon, and was overcome with a sense of God's
greatness: "O Lord our Lord, how excellent is thy name in all the
earth! . . . When I consider thy heavens, the work of thy fingers,
the moon and the stars, which thou hast ordained; What is man,

that thou art mindful of him?" (PSALM 8:1, 3, 4). That's a good question—What is man? It is a question all of us ought to consider.

√ Back in 1926 a chemist decided he would analyze the human body in order to discover its commercial value. He discovered that if you weigh 160 pounds, and are five feet ten inches tall, your body contains enough iron to make one nail; enough phosphorus to make 2,200 match heads; enough fat to make seven bars of soap; enough sugar to fill a small dish; enough lime to whitewash a chicken coop; and a little magnesium, potassium, and sulphur left over. The commercial value of all this was 98 cents back in 1926. Due to inflation, and on today's market, you would be worth about two dollars.

√ Is that all there is to man? No person in his right mind would put himself up for sale at such a price. You are made in the image of God, and you can be filled with the Spirit of God, and you are here to do God's will. To believe this about man makes a big difference.

What a man believes about himself will determine how he lives. If you are dust, and only dust, why not have your fling and satisfy the desires of the flesh? If you are only dust, go ahead—eat, drink, and be merry. Live the way you want to. But give everybody else the same privilege you take for yourself.

√ Man is more than flesh, blood, and bone. There is something deep within the soul of man that calls to us. It calls us to stand tall, walk straight, and live unselfishly. Until we respond to that call, we can never be happy. Unless we live by some sort of moral compass, we will soon be lost in a world of hopelessness.

A young man was brought before a judge to be sentenced for a crime for which he had been convicted. The judge saw some good qualities in the boy and talked to him in his private chamber. "Tell me, son, why did you do it?" The boy replied, "I guess I just lived up to what people expected me to do." Our children sometimes do the things they think we expect them to do. Well, God expects us to attain a spiritual level of living that most of us have not yet attained.

· 122 ·

A few days ago I ran out of gas. Fortunately I was in front of a service station. It doesn't take much city driving before your tank is empty. You may have the finest car money can buy, but unless you keep gasoline in the tank, you don't have transportation. Today's automobiles will not run on kerosene or diesel fuel; they are made for gasoline.

You may fill your days with fun and frolic, but your soul remains empty until you open your heart to God. The circumstances around your life may be exactly what you want, but the soul remains dull and lifeless until you accept God as your partner.

√ Dr. Ellis Fuller once preached a sermon on the far country. One normally thinks of the far country as a desolate place where the scum of society have settled. It's easy to think of the far country in the words of Kipling: "Where the trails run out and stop." Dr. Fuller said the far country is "Anywhere . . . a man tries to live without God." That's a good definition. The far country could be the house in which I live, or the one next door. It could be on the loveliest street in the city where the lawns are trimmed and the houses are decorated with sparkling chandeliers. When a man fails to follow the footsteps of God, he is already in the far country. He doesn't have to wait until his bank account is exhausted and there are patches on his pants and holes in his shoes.

⌐When life appears meaningless, remember your heritage. It is a marvelous thought to know that you were made in the image of God. You may feel defeated, but you have tremendous possibilities. Don't let life defeat you. Remember, you are a child of the King. If you believe that, then act as if you do.

There always seems to be a breakdown of morals during the crisis of war. On hearing of the immorality between American soldiers and German girls, a father was concerned about his son, who was stationed in Germany. When the boy came home, the father said, "Son, I've got to know. Did you follow the crowd?" The young man looked his dad in the face, and replied, "Dad, don't you know that there are some things men with our name can be trusted not to do?" That was all the answer the father needed.

There are some things that you can trust people not to do if they bear the name of Christ. They will not cheat. They will not lie. They will not take unfair advantage of another.

Remember Susan Warner's book *The End of a Coil,* in which Rupert and Dolly visited the ruins of Rome? Dolly reminded Rupert that most of the emperors of Rome died a violent death. They were murdered or committed suicide. "Some were really great men, weren't they?" asked Rupert. "Here is Trajan," said Dolly. "He was a philosopher and a distinguished man in the arts of war and peace. Yet, he ordered any who professed Christianity to be put to death. Do you think he was great in the sight of God? Here is Marcus Aurelius. He was what the world calls a very great man. He was wise, strong and cultivated. He sought out Christians, east and west, and had them tortured and killed. What do you think the Lord thinks of such greatness?"

"Well," asked Rupert, "what is greatness? What is worth trying to achieve?" "Only that which will last," answered Dolly. "What will last?" asked Rupert. "Only the work you do for God." "But what about all the other work we do?" questioned Rupert. "All our work should be done for God," Dolly replied. "The merchant ought to make money for His service. The lawyer ought to bring justice to all; break every yoke; let the oppressed go free. Soldiers ought to fight to protect the weak people from violence and wrong."

"Why should a man try to improve himself?" asked Rupert. "So he can serve God better," Dolly answered. "If you are right," Rupert said, "then the rest of the world is wrong." "Yes," Dolly replied, "the Bible says: 'The wrong way is the broad way where most of the people go.'"

When life seems hopeless, remember that God is not only your Creator, but that He is with you. Jesus said, ". . . with God all things are possible" (MATTHEW 19:26). This is a daring faith. What did Jesus mean? Surely He meant that no situation is hopeless. Certainly He meant that no matter what the circumstances of life are, we can be victorious. Above all, He meant that human personality does not travel a dead-end road. It runs through deep waters and up steep mountains, but at the end of the journey there is light and peace for those who have been faithful to God.

The psalmist learned the truth of this point a long time ago. It is reflected in his wise words: "Yea, though I walk through the valley of the shadow of death, I will fear no evil: for thou art with me . . ." (PSALM 23:4). There is no way around that valley, but His is a hand that will keep us steady as we make the journey.

There is a story about Billy Hicks, a petty officer in the British Navy. He was finally promoted to the captain of the foretop. He knew it was a dangerous post and that two men who had held the post had fallen to their death. Billy was afraid.

A few nights before he was to assume his new post, Billy was seen working with the signal apparatus as if he were sending an urgent message. When he was to make his first climb, he went aloft like a seasoned sailor and came down safely. He was a changed man, but no one knew why.

The secret of his transformation was not discovered until an officer of another vessel was a guest on board. The guest asked the captain if he had a man on board by the name of Billy Hicks. When the captain told him he did, the visitor said he had noticed a signal coming from the ship and had asked his signal officer to take down the message. This was the message:

"God, this is Billy Hicks speaking. I'm not afraid of no living man. . . . I'm not asking for any special favors except one. . . . When I climb the foretop tomorrow, let it be with the courage of a man who is clean. And, O God, if it's just the same with You, from this day on, give me the feeling I used to have long ago when I knelt at my mother's knee and said, 'Our Father. . . .' Good night, God."

Life is hopeless without God. With God, the burdens of life can be endured, and you and I can be triumphant.

On my way to the church one day, I heard a new song; or at least it was the first time I had heard it. It was entitled "Life Is Empty Without You." The writer was not thinking of theology when he penned those lines, but if you think of human life in relation to God, there is some mighty good theology in those words. Life never loses its meaning if you feel the touch of God's hand, and if you believe that He is the creator and the Goal of life.

15

Take a Look at Yourself

"What do you like most about your work?" a friend asked. "I love to preach most," was my reply.

Week after week and year after year, the minister stands behind the pulpit to speak to his people. He has a marvelous opportunity as well as a tremendous responsibility. There is always the temptation to echo the mind of the congregation. One is likely to get the feeling that some people are interested in hearing about the sins of other generations, but have no interest in exposing the sins of our society. The minister who is true to his calling must get his message from God and speak clearly and profoundly to those who sit in the pews each Sunday. If his message comes from God, he will hit his target Sunday after Sunday. God does not require us to be successful, but He does demand that we be faithful.

There was a preacher who went to serve a new congregation, and he called a meeting of his officials soon after arriving. The officials seemed eager to assist the preacher by suggesting certain subjects that should not be expounded in his new parish. "Don't say anything about liquor," one suggested, "because one of our largest contributors owns the biggest still in these parts. Don't talk about gambling, because some of your prominent members have a little poker game each week." "I would advise," said another, "that you go easy on the subject of gossip, because this is a prevailing pastime in this town." The startled preacher asked, "What on earth can I preach?" "I know," exclaimed one member;

"Talk about the Jews. There isn't one in a hundred miles of this place."

Jesus was a successful preacher because He spoke to the needs of people in a language they could understand. You cannot separate the teachings of Jesus from life.

Every sermon ought to do at least two things: it must magnify man's weakness, and remind him of his need for redemption; then it must bring man to the place where he can see the greatness of God and His eagerness to help. As a minister, I feel compelled to remind people that a new birth is necessary if we are to reach the destiny for which God created us. The minister will denounce some things, but he must be careful not to remain too long in valleys of denunciation. He must warn us of impending dangers and decry the evil that parades in garments of respectability and social charm. He must not only talk of the dark and evil night through which we pass, but he must tell of a morning that is possible.

The minister is charged with the awesome responsibility to proclaim the Good News. Now comes the big question: What is the Good News? The most thrilling news I know is that Christ died for our sins. Jesus gave us a grand picture of God's character, and everywhere in His teachings we see evidence of a good God who stands ready to forgive us. The life and death of Jesus also express the fact that you and I, through daily communion with God, can overcome all the evil that plagues us.

Another great challenge in preaching is to keep people growing in the Christian faith. You may be able to read music, but that will never assure you of being an accomplished musician unless you pay the price of long hours of practice. You may plant the finest rose bushes available, but you cannot expect to enjoy a beautiful rose garden without keeping the weeds pulled up. You may go to the altar and respond to the marriage vows with a heart full of dreams, but your noble hopes will turn to gray ashes unless you keep the fires of love burning and work to fulfill your dreams. You can walk around in the woods with a perfectly good compass in your pocket and remain lost unless you have learned to use it.

You and I must sit at the feet of the Master and learn the lessons of life that will enable us to be victorious in facing the little irritating cares, as well as the great tragedies, that lie in the future.

A good deal of preaching must be directed to those who have set sail on the sea of Christian living, but who still need words of courage to keep moving. Suppose you were to go to see your physician while in great pain. You might even feel that death might be near. Your physician examines you and then says very gently, "You are a mighty sick man." You wait for a word of hope and, after a long silence the doctor repeats his first statement: "You are a mighty sick man." You might respond by saying, "Yes, doctor, I know that, but is there anything you can do to help me?" You would not be interested in hearing how sick you were; you would be eager to know if there was a prescription that would make you well again.

Jesus never left anyone without a word of hope. Even the rich young man who came to inquire about eternal life was assured of an open door through which he could walk. The young man had permitted wealth to build a wall between God and himself. No matter what difficult problem we are facing, there is always hope, because with God all things are possible. Preaching must wave a flag of hope before a weary humanity.

While walking through a crowded department store, I noticed a little boy crying. I walked over and stooped down before him and asked him to tell me why he was crying. "I can't find my father," he said. "Don't you cry," I said to him, "and I'll help you find your father." That brought him courage and he dried his tears as we headed toward the Lost and Found Department. Little help I would have been had I said to him, "Son, you are lost, and that's too bad. Maybe you will never find your father." When we reached the Lost and Found Department, there was his father. The man gathered his little boy in his arms and said, "I'm sorry you got lost. I have been looking everywhere for you. From now on, you must let me hold your hand."

We often get lost, and perhaps it's because we do not want the

Father to hold us by the hand. We want to walk alone and do as we please. Like the little boy, if we let God hold us by the hand, we will never get lost. Jesus is constantly saying to us, "Come with Me, and I'll show you the Father."

God doesn't take our human freedom away once we are saved. We are not mere puppets on a string, in spite of the fact that we have surrendered our wills to Him. We can still deny God and refuse to do His will. We can, by sheer selfishness, push Him from the throne of our lives and give Mr. Ego control again.

Let me suggest three simple steps that will lead you to a new life:

(1) Don't be afraid to admit that you have been wrong. Once a man called me and asked if I would talk to his son. "Tell me," I asked, "what seems to be the trouble?" "He thinks he knows everything, and that he is never wrong. Just tell him that everybody is wrong sometimes." There is no help for the person who refuses to admit he is wrong. You can't help such a person because he doesn't even recognize the problem, let alone feel the need for help.

In counseling with couples who are drifting on the sea of domestic storms, I know my job is a difficult one, if not impossible, when two people come in and tell me that the trouble does not lie with either of them. When a woman tells me all the fault is with her husband, and when her husband tells me it is all his wife's fault, I know there isn't much help I can offer until they are able to see their own mistakes. Admitting your faults is the first step in becoming the person you can become.

(2) Ask God to forgive you. There is no record of anyone being turned away who has come to God forsaking his sins and seeking forgiveness. Dr. James McConnell of Oklahoma City told a story many years ago about a day when he was fishing on the Missouri River. Dr. McConnell looked up and saw a small boy frantically waving a red flag from a homemade dock jutting out into the river. He also saw a large Missouri River steamboat coming down the river. It looked as if the boy might be trying to stop that boat, so Dr. McConnell moved down to where the boy

stood and asked, "You don't mean to tell me that you are fool enough to think that great riverboat will respond to your signal and try to stop at this little dock on the bend of the river?" "Sure I do, mister," the boy replied confidently, "it'll stop, all right. It'll stop." "That boat couldn't possible stop in this swift water, even if the Captain wanted to stop," Dr. McConnell answered. "They'll stop, all right, mister, they'll stop. I ain't afraid they won't stop!" Just then, Dr. McConnell saw the great boat make a sudden swerve and heard the whistle blow twice in recognition of the boy's signal. The steamboat slowly made its way over to the boy's homemade dock and the gangplank was run out and the boy stepped on board. He looked back over his shoulder at the stranger and said, "I ain't no fool, mister. My father's captain of this boat!" Need any more be said? You wave your little flag and ask God to forgive you, and He will. I have never been more sure of anything in my life.

(3) You must believe on the Lord Jesus Christ. Remember the story of Paul and Silas having been cast into prison because they were accused of disturbing the peace and teaching customs that were unlawful for the Romans to follow. After they were publicly beaten, they were thrown in what would be called a "maximum security" prison, and the jailer was sternly charged to see that they did not escape. At midnight, while the prisoners were praying and singing, an earthquake shattered the prison doors and every prisoner could have walked to freedom. The Philippian jailer awakened and drew his sword to kill himself, supposing the prisoners had escaped. Paul urged him to keep calm and assured him that all prisoners were present and accounted for. The jailer was afraid that he would be put to death if the prisoners escaped. He came trembling to Paul and Silas and fell on his knees and asked, "Sirs, what must I do to be saved?" They replied, "Believe on the Lord Jesus Christ, and thou shalt be saved . . ." (ACTS 16:30-31).

Now just what does that mean? Does it mean that we are to give intellectual assent to Jesus? Many people believe that Jesus lived, but mere belief has made little or no difference in their lives. Look up the word *believe*. It means to "accept," to "have faith in," and to "trust." To believe on the Lord Jesus Christ is a transforming experience. It means living by His teachings and following in His footsteps. Polycarp, a first-century Christian, expressed this belief when men were being fed to the lions and burned at the stake for their faith. He was arrested and asked to denounce Christ. The Roman officer who arrested Polycarp tried to persuade him to say, "Lord Caesar." Polycarp said, "I am a Christian." "Just pay your respect to Caesar and save your life," the proconsul urged; "Reproach Christ and you will be free." Polycarp said, "Eighty and six years have I served Him and He never did me an injury; how, then, can I blaspheme my King and my Saviour?" He was led to the stake and burned alive. Never once did he flinch from the pain. That is what Paul meant by believing. We must trust and follow.

To believe on Jesus is more than a mere tip of the hat on Sunday; it is taking hold of His hand and walking confidently through life with Him. To believe on Jesus is to trust Him when the shadows fall around us; it is to believe that He is a true revelation of God's character, and that His life expresses God's care and concern for us. It is to believe that through Him we can be redeemed, and by His example we can meet all the problems of life successfully. To believe on Jesus is to follow Him through the dark tunnels of suffering and through the deep valleys of sorrow and disappointment, knowing that on some tomorrow He will bring us to the sunlit hills of that land where sorrows are not known, suffering is only a faint memory, and disappointments are forgotten.

Let God's love flow through your life. God's love is deep and unfathomable. Human love is often shallow and superficial. Divine love moves in three directions: from God to man; from man to God; from man to man. Every man's life is either a channel for God's love or a stuffy storage bin for his own selfish desires. When we commit ourselves to God, life becomes a rippling stream as His love flows through our thoughts, deeds, and attitudes. If we fail to commit ourselves to Him, life becomes a pond stagnant with the stench of egotism, covered with the slime of selfishness.

It is thrilling to know that God can live within us. Paul expressed this when He exclaimed, "I am crucified with Christ: nevertheless I live; yet not I, but Christ liveth in me . . ." (GALATIANS 2:20). Jesus talked about this idea when He said, "As the Father hath loved me, so have I loved you: continue ye in my love" (JOHN 15:9).

Jesus knew that it was man's nature to love himself. Therefore, He never commanded us to love ourselves; but He did say, "Thou shalt love thy neighbour as thyself" (MATTHEW 22:39). He did not condemn man's love for himself. To care for ourselves is not necessarily evil, but to exclude others from the same concern and love we express for ourselves is wrong. Our greatest problem is not the task of loving ourselves. Our great challenge lies in loving ourselves in the right way, and loving others in the light of the teachings of our Lord.

A woman writes, "How can we know that God's love is within us?" There is only one answer to that question. Jesus gave us the answer on two different occasions. Once He said, "By this shall all men know that ye are my disciples, if ye have love one to another" (JOHN 13:35). A man can shout all day that he loves God with all his heart, but unless that love moves in the direction of his fellow man, you can be sure that God's love fails to flow through his life. Jesus also said, ". . . the tree is known by his fruit" (MATTHEW 12:33). A good tree will bring forth good fruit, and man will reap what he sows. That is God's law in nature as well as in the spirit.

When we relate ourselves properly to God, all our human relationships will be Christian. The kind of love we express for one another depends upon the degree to which we love God. It follows that the evidence of our love for God will be expressed in the way we treat our fellow man.

Once a young man in a Midwestern city decided to leave home. He announced his intentions to his father and advised him that he would be leaving the next morning. "I have decided to leave," he said; "I am tired of your restraints and mother's piety." The night was long and restless for that father and mother. They loved their son and were afraid of what might happen to him in a large city without their Christian counsel. All night they turned restlessly and the stains of many tears were on the pillows.

The next morning they heard their son tiptoeing down the stairs an hour before he usually arose. The father jumped out of bed and went to the head of the stairs and called out to the boy who had already reached the front door. "Son, come in here for a moment!" The boy turned back and walked slowly to his parents' room. His father put his arm gently but firmly around the boy's shoulder and said, "Son, your mother and I have not slept all night. We are sure that there must be something wrong in our lives, and before you go we want to ask you to forgive us." The boy looked into the weather-beaten face of his father and saw the tears of love on his cheeks. "Father," the boy said, "the trouble is not with you and mother; the trouble is with me." Together they knelt by the bed and prayed. The boy got up with God's love flowing in his life. After that, home was the happiest place in the world for him.

16

Life Can Be Better

Some people are asking profound and significant questions: Where is God? How can I relate my life to Him? Can I be triumphant? Does my life have an eternal purpose?

I received an astounding letter recently from an academic dean in one of our great universities. He had read something I had written which was obviously basic in Christian tradition, and he wrote: "I'm glad to know that somebody still believes in the fundamental teachings of Jesus. I have just returned from a worship service in which I heard an eloquent preacher deliver a sermon, with proficient dullness, on psychological vibrations."

That phrase "proficient dullness" caught my eye. It reminded me of a story I heard some years ago. A pastoral relations committee asked for a new preacher on the grounds that the one they had was supernaturally dull. The bishop wanted to know what they meant by the term "supernaturally dull." "Well," said the spokesman for the committee, "no man could be as dull as our preacher without divine aid."

Man estranged from God is like a mighty ship without a captain. The potentialities are gigantic, but the ship sails to no harbor, delivers no cargo, carries no passengers, and reaches no destination without a captain. Without God, man drifts in a sea of frustration and uncertainty with his cargo of selfishness. The challenge of preaching has never been greater, and the harvest to garner has never been larger than it is in our generation.

Dorothy Sayers released a stinging indictment against those of us who stand in the pulpits of the nation when she wrote, "You have the greatest good news on earth—the incarnation of God in human life—and you treat it as an insignificant news item, fit for page fourteen in the chronicle of daily events." That is a scathing remark, but the tragedy lies in the fact that there is more truth in it than we ministers wish to admit. We must be alive to the needs of our people and also aware of the power of God to meet those needs.

Ministers must do more than proclaim the news events of the week or denounce the evil that surrounds us. We need to lift up Christ, who is the only Light that flickers in our dark world. We can get the news on TV, but it doesn't motivate us to make better news tomorrow. We can read fresh reports of what is happening in our world in the daily paper, but it is never redemptive. Preaching ought to be like a candle burning in a dark night, or like a drink of fresh water found in the midst of a parched desert.

Remember the words of the psalmist, as translated by Moffatt, "When I was hemmed in, Thou hast freed me often" (PSALM 4:1). Well, a lot of people are hemmed in today. They are hemmed in by their sins. They are hemmed in by their selfishness and disappointment. They are hemmed in by their fears and sorrows. The Good News we have to proclaim is that God can free them.

Catherine Marshall talked about that feeling of being hemmed in when her husband died. God can take the worst situation and make something good out of it. Calvary and the ugly deeds performed there were transformed into a place where all men can find the forgiveness they do not deserve. When Peter Marshall died, a prophetic voice was silenced at the age of forty-six. Catherine Marshall wrote: "On that chilly January morning in 1949—as I looked at my husband's face for the last time, then turned to leave the bare little hospital room—it seemed like whistling in the dark, to believe that God could bring good out of such tragic loss." She found release from that feeling, and through her writings has been able to minister to the needs of others.

Joseph R. Sizoo, in his book *Still We Can Hope*, tells us about the professor who was a brilliant Greek scholar and a wonderful interpreter of the New Testament. Once he taught a course on the Book of Romans. When he came to the eighth chapter of Romans, the grand old professor read that strange verse, "All things work together for good to them that love God." One of the students lifted his hand, and when the professor recognized him, he inquired, "Professor, you do not mean to tell us that a man with your intellect believes that?" "Yes," the professor replied, "I believe it with all my heart." Later in the afternoon, the professor and his wife went for a ride in their automobile. There was a terrible crash that left the professor unconscious and his wife dead. When the old scholar became conscious, he was in a hospital. A nurse stood nearby, and the professor asked her if she would telephone and ask the president of the institution in which he taught to come to see him. When the president entered the room, the professor said, "Tell my class what I said this morning about ROMANS 8:28 still holds good." Then he died.

Remember the agonizing prayer our Lord prayed under the shadow of the olive trees in the Garden of Gethsemane: ". . . nevertheless not my will, but thine, be done" (LUKE 22:42). Follow Him for a few minutes to the praetorium. Hear again the false accusations brought against Him. Watch Him stagger under the weight of the cross. Listen to Him pray. ". . . My God, my God, why hast thou forsaken me?" (MARK 15:34). Ask yourself the question: "Does His prayer in the Garden still hold good?" Sensitive hearts can hear Him whisper above the noise of gambling soldiers, "Father, what I said in the Garden of Gethsemane still holds good." All of us get hemmed in now and then, but we can be set free by the grace and power of God. That's Good News!

E. Stanley Jones once told a story about a Danish wood-carver who picked up a piece of driftwood along the shore in Hawaii and, seeing its possibilities, carved a beautiful head of Christ. Without God, we are little more than driftwood on the restless shores of eternity, but God sees within each one of us a faithful disciple.

In the powerful little parable of the lost sheep, Jesus gives us a word picture of the pursuing love of God. He comes to us; He dogs our steps until we invite Him to live within. When we clog our souls with cheap deeds and waste our efforts in selfish pursuits, He knows that we could yet become obedient sons of God.

The major thrust of this parable is twofold: (1) God's ceaseless love for an undeserving humanity, and (2) man's need for redemption. Not only do we see the wonder of God's love, but the hopelessness of man ever finding his way back to the fold by himself.

A hundred sheep would have been a large flock in Palestine during the time in which Jesus lived. Yet the loss of even one animal would have sent a good shepherd into the wilderness to search for it. A shepherd with less concern might have been pleased to keep ninety-nine percent of his sheep. He might even have rejoiced in the fact that only one was missing.

In America, the average congregation has about twenty-five percent of the members present on a given Sunday. That leaves seventy-five percent of the flock unaccounted for. What is our attitude? How do we react? Do we say to ourselves, "Let them find their way back," or "They should know better than to stay away"? Or do we just forget them and, after a reasonable length of time, mark them off the records or place them on the inactive role?

Once a mother who had a rather large number of children was being interviewed by a newspaper reporter. He asked, "Which one do you love the most?" She was a wise woman and her reply indicated not only her wisdom, but a good mother's spirit. "I love the one most who is away from home until he returns; and the one who is sick until he is well; and the one who is hurt until the hurt disappears; and the one who is lost until he is found." Some scholars tell us that the sheepfold in which the shepherds herded the sheep at night was shaped like the capital letter "C"; and the shepherd wrapped himself in his garments when the shadows fell, and slept across the opening so that any animal that tried to ravage the flock first had to encounter the shepherd. What a grand picture of the shepherd! It reminds me of the words, "I am the good shepherd, . . . I lay down my life for the sheep" (JOHN 10:14-15).

There is a dramatic scene in Ian Maclaren's book *Beside the Bonnie Brier Bush* which relates the story of Flora Campbell running away from home. Flora's father, Lachlan, was deeply hurt and he struck her name from the family Bible. When Marget Howe came to talk to Lachlan, she found him hard, cold, and stubborn. "She is not anything to me," said Lachlan, ". . . she has been a black shame to her name . . . would to God that she was lying in the graveyard."

Marget Howe spoke softly, but firmly, "Just twenty years ago this spring her mother died. Not a woman to watch over her and she wandered from the fold, and all you can do is to take her out of your Bible. Woe is me if our Father had blotted out our names from the Book of Life when we left His house. But He sent His Son to seek us, an' a weary road He came. I tell you, a man wouldn't leave a sheep to perish as you have cast your child away."

Before many minutes had passed, Lachlan was on his knees, praying, "God be merciful to me a sinner." After addressing a letter Marget had written, begging Flora to return home, Lachlan cleaned the lamp that had been kept for show and had never been used, and he placed it in the window each evening. Every night its light shone down the steep path to Flora's home like the divine love from the open door of our Father's house.

Here is a question we should consider: How can we become more effective in our witness for Christ? We need to possess more fully three indelible qualities we see so clearly etched in the life of our Lord:

(1) Notice the unflinching allegiance Christ had for His Father. Jesus had but one purpose: He wanted to please His Father and live God's will to perfection in His own life.

After a long, weary day, Jesus sat by Jacob's well and talked with a woman about living water, which she so desperately needed. The disciples had gone into the city to buy meat, and when they returned they begged Jesus to eat. He said, "My meat is to do the will of him that sent me, and to finish his work" (JOHN 4:34). Let us be careful that our purpose does not become cloudy with activities other than the Master's work.

Harold Bosley, in his book *The Mind of Christ,* opens his first chapter with a delightful little story that suggests the Christian strategy we need to follow. A missionary, who had just arrived at a new post in China, asked a little girl, who had been picked up as an orphan and cared for in the mission, whether or not she had heard the gospel. "No," she replied, "but I have seen it." Aye, that is far better than hearing the gospel. We ought to live such a life that others can see the gospel in us.

Jesus Christ was and is the gospel. Those who flocked around Him could see it at work in His attitudes as well as in His deeds of love. This day requires the church not only to proclaim the gospel, but to be the gospel.

(2) Notice the discipline Christ demanded of Himself. The work of His Father had priority in His life; it was always God first. Jesus studied the scripture and was often found at the place of prayer.

E. Stanley Jones tells the story of a monk coming to his abbot and saying, "I do not know what is wrong with me. I keep the rules, I fast at all appointed times. I pray according to the prescribed regulations for perfect monks. And yet, I am a complete failure. What is the matter with me?" The abbot lifted two fingers toward the sun until the monk noticed the light filtering through his fingers as red as blood itself. Then the abbot spoke: "You must become a flame of fire." That's the secret. Those of us who stand in the pulpits, and those who wave His banners and profess Him as Lord, must become flames of fire before our influence can be what it ought to be.

I am thrilled every time I read that story of the old slum woman who sat, Sunday after Sunday, in the congregation George Matheson once served. For a long time she had lived in a cellar. One day, to the astonishment of her neighbors, she moved from the dark, dingy cellar to a sunny garret. When her friends assailed her with questions, she answered, "You cannot hear George Matheson preach, and live in a cellar."

Every preacher who reads these lines could be a better preacher if he demanded more of himself. Everyday, when I look into the mirror to shave, I say to myself, "Bob Ozment, you could be a better preacher." To believe otherwise is to stop growing. Every layman whose eyes fall across these pages could have a greater influence for good on others if he demanded more of himself. The world is full of people who live in damp cellars. Your preaching and the way you live could cause them to change their residency.

(3) Notice the unfaltering compassion Jesus had for others. The Master loved people, not because of what they were, but because of what He knew they could become. It's easy to love nice people who do nice things for you. Such love is rooted in selfishness. God's love breaks through the bands of hostility and prejudice to love us for what we can become when we are fully consecrated to Him. I can think of a thousand reasons why I love my Saviour, but I cannot think of a single reason why He should love me.

When our Lord's fame spread throughout the land, He went from city to city and taught the multitudes and healed their diseases. He saw great numbers of people with so many burdens and hurts. Their lives had neither purpose nor direction. The writer of Matthew says, ". . . he was moved with compassion . . . because they . . . were scattered abroad, as sheep having no shepherd" (MATTHEW 9:36).

We can never earn His grace; neither can we deserve His forgiveness nor merit His love. Nevertheless they are ours. His grace is extended to our hearts, His love surrounds us; and when we turn from our sins, His forgiveness is ours.

Francis Bourdillon wrote:

> The mind has a thousand eyes,
> And the heart but one;

Yet the light of a whole life dies,
When love is done.

"Light"

There is a story about a Negro slave standing on the deck of a sinking ship with what looked like a heavy bundle in his arms. He was about to step aboard a lifeboat already overcrowded when a member of the crew shouted, "Come ahead, but leave the bundle behind. There is not enough room for both you and whatever you have in the bundle." The old Negro pressed the bundle to his bosom and opened its folds. There lay two small children who had been committed to his care. He kissed them and lowered them into the boat with this request: "Tell the master that I was faithful in fulfilling his charge." The boat pushed away and the dark man stood alone on the deck of the sinking ship. That's fidelity! That's discipline! That's love!

That is really a parable of Jesus staggering up the cruel slopes of Calvary. The cross was a heavy burden, but Jesus was convinced that it was God's Way, and He was determined to be faithful. Listen to those agonizing words of victory as Jesus shouts, with the last ounce of energy, "It is finished" (JOHN 19:30). What did He mean? Did He mean only that a difficult ordeal had come to an end? Did He mean that the dying note of His earthly symphony was fading away? No! He meant that His work was finished, and that His life had been lived in perfect harmony with the will of God. Another translation might read, "Father, I was faithful in fulfilling the charge committed to me."

Have we been faithful? Have we stood the test of living up to God's expectations of us?

17

Don't Be Afraid of Tomorrow

Bishop Arthur J. Moore, in his book *Fight On! Fear Not!*, reminds us of the divine power that can be ours during life's most difficult battles: "Christ does not take us out of the battle: He does something better. He gives us trust and triumph in the battle and promises that, at the end of the struggle, a friendly hand will guide us into the presence of One Whose 'Well done, thou good and faithful servant,' will glorify the battle scars."

On his eighty-seventh birthday, Carl Sandburg said to a group of reporters, "Life is short. You'd better resolve that it is short." The swiftness of our earthly journey is frightening to some. I wish the poet had elaborated on his remark. He was reminding us to live each day fully, and to make every stroke on the canvas of life count. We have learned an important lesson when we discover that life is too short to be selfish, stubborn, and little. William Thackeray wrote, "Life is a mirror: if you frown at it, it frowns back: If you smile, it returns the greeting." That is not a new principle. Paul wrote in his letter to the Galatians: "Be not deceived; God is not mocked: for whatsoever a man soweth, that shall he also reap" (GALATIANS 6:7).

Mr. Sandburg could have said, "Life will bring sorrow, hurt, and disappointment. You'd better resolve that in your heart." I am sure of one thing: Man does not fail because life is hard; neither does man succeed because life is easy. The circumstances of life are beside the point. Man is driven to defeat and despair, or he climbs to the peaks of joy and triumph because of his attitude toward life and his faith in God.

God offers to every man the strength he must have in order to bear his load. The man who refuses that strength will be crushed, but the man who accepts it will be triumphant. Let me tell you about two men with whom I have been counseling in recent months. Both of them have been brought low by the problems they face. They are passing slowly and painfully through a dark valley. One man feels the hopelessness of utter despair; he believes that the only way out of his present misery is suicide. He is unwilling to face the consequences of his ugly sins. There can be no help for him until he commits himself to God. The other man has asked God for help, and while the night is still dark, he is marching toward the sunlit mountains of victory. Here are two men walking in the dark night of life. One man feels the heavy hammer of defeat, while the other holds tenaciously to the hand of God.

One of my ambitions has been to play the piano. I realize that I will never achieve that goal. To become an accomplished musician demands a lot of time, and I do not feel that I can afford the time it requires. It has been said that life is very much like a piano. One man sits at the keyboard and runs his fingers over the keys in a haphazard way. His efforts produce harsh music filled with discord that is unpleasant to the ear. Another man touches the keys with the hands of a master musician and sends out a succession of melodious sounds that are soothing to the ear. Both men use the same instrument, but one man produces discord while the other produces harmony. Of course, the difference is found in the fact that one man knows little about music, while the other has spent years learning to play the piano correctly. You see, it is what you bring to the keyboard of life that makes the difference.

Life is the same way. Live it according to the teachings of the Master, and it gives you harmony. Live it in the name of selfishness, and it produces discord. No intelligent person would say the piano is at fault when harsh notes are heard; and we cannot honestly say that life is at fault when the storms descend upon us.

Do you remember that thrilling story of the Israelites leaving Egypt under the leadership of Moses? What a magnificent sight it must have been to watch that nation leave a land in which they had been enslaved, to march toward the Promised Land upon which the eyes of the Lord gazed constantly. The air must have been electrified with excitement as the people marched triumphantly out of slavery. It was not long, however, before the Israelites became discontented with their position. Whenever they confronted danger or suffered the hardships of life, they complained. Soon after they left Egypt and faced their first crisis, they murmured, "Let us alone, that we may serve the Egyptians . . . better for us to serve the Egyptians, than that we should die in the wilderness" (EXODUS 14:12).

Humanity tends to suffer from a chronic disease of complaining. Doubts concerning God's care and goodness arise, when life is hard and burdens are heavy. We often question the wisdom of God when the future is blurred and circumstances place upon us the crushing sorrows of life. When the Israelites complained, Moses, their stalwart leader, said, "Fear ye not, stand still, and see the salvation of the Lord . . ." (EXODUS 14:13).

Moses preached a mighty powerful sermon in that one statement: (1) He was saying, "Don't be afraid. Don't give up and turn back." (2) He was urging the people to stand still—"Get hold of yourself. Let's take a good look at the problem before we quit." (3) He was reminding the people to trust God.

When your troubles seem more than you can bear, remember the advice of Moses: master your fears, stand still, and look to God for the strength you need. For those who are faithful, God will provide the strength that is necessary to ring the bells of victory when they reach the end of their earthly journey.

The person who feels the gentle tug of God's hand will never be afraid on the road of life. Mrs. Carl Simon tells us a delightful story that illustrates this truth. When Mrs. Simon was a little

girl, one thing to which she looked forward was a Sunday afternoon walk with the family. Often they would walk down along
the railroad track into a lovely wooded area. There they would
run and play, and in the spring they picked fragrant wildflowers.
Like most journeys through life, there are always some unpleasant places through which we must pass. In order to get to the
woods in which they played, it was necessary for the family to
cross a high trestle that spanned a creek. The children would
often run ahead of the parents, but Mrs. Simon said, "I always
waited for my father a few feet this side of the trestle. I didn't
dare cross it without him. Often my brothers would offer me their
hand, but I did not want to walk with them. I wanted my father.
With my hand in his, I stepped confidently across those ties with
no sense of fear, knowing that he would guide me safely to the
other side."

Before the children of Israel entered the Promised Land, Moses
tried to impress upon them the importance of keeping the commandments. The theology one is likely to read in Moses' charge
to obey the Lord might be expressed as follows: be good; keep
God's commandments, and everything will be fine. Moses promised Israel that, as long as they loved and served God, the fields
would yield a good harvest and grass would grow for the cattle.
On the other hand, if they followed a false god, the rains would
cease, the fields would not yield their harvest, and the grass
would fail to grow. It does not take one long to conclude that the
good are not always rich and the rich are not always good. God
does not always reward righteousness with good health and
material wealth. If He did, I know a lot of people who would be
more regular in church attendance.

There is a truth we can draw from this theological interpretation of Moses' words. We are all completely dependent upon
the goodness and mercy of God, and to become aware of God's
love and goodness will result in our keeping His commandments.
To live otherwise spells spiritual disaster.

Jesus warned us not to be overly concerned about acquiring the
material things of life. These are not really important when we

see them in the light of eternal values. Do not worry about the clothes you wear or the food you need. God takes care of the lilies of the field and the birds of the air, and we can trust Him to take care of us. Jesus challenged us to "seek ye first the kingdom of God, and his righteousness; and all these things shall be added unto you" (MATTHEW 6:33).

Our Lord knew that we would be tempted to give priority to material things and neglect spiritual matters. All of us would agree that Jesus had a keen insight into human nature. I know people who are spending most of their time and energy with one goal in mind: the acquisition of things. They live in beautiful houses, buy exquisite foods, wrap themselves in the latest fashions while their souls starve for Christian nurture and shiver in the cold shacks of spiritual poverty. Whatever else the Master meant by "All these things shall be added unto you," He expressed His faith in the adequacy of God's power.

Jesus was suggesting that many of us live as if we were alone in the world without the sustaining presence of the God who loves us and who will take care of us. God provides, for those who love and serve Him, the necessary material out of which they can build victorious lives. Most of us are endowed with material blessings that we do not need, but few of us are overstocked with spiritual strength and fortitude.

There are three things Moses challenged the Israelites to do; they are also a challenge for us: (1) love the Lord; (2) walk in all His ways; (3) cleave unto Him.

I have never known a person who loved God, who walked in His holy ways, and who held to the hem of His garment, to be deserted by the Father and allowed to sink to the depths of despair. The psalmist expressed it this way: "I have been young, and now am old; yet have I not seen the righteous forsaken, nor his seed begging bread" (PSALM 37:25). God will never forsake us.

I talk with many people who are afraid of tomorrow. Fear of the future will paralyze us and keep us from present duties as well as rob us of the hopes that thrill the soul. The general rule usually follows that one who is afraid of tomorrow has failed to walk with God in the past and refused to give life his best; therefore, he cannot trust God for the future. To say it in a positive way, I have never known one to carry a big bag of fears in his heart if he has walked with God, given his best to the duties of today, and anchored his faith in God.

When Moses challenged the Israelities to walk without fear, he reminded them of God's goodness in the past. When fear fills our minds, let us remember the past. You may be worried, and perhaps you have good reason to worry, but I challenge you to sit down and write the things that worried you five years ago. I doubt that you will be able to think of many things to write down, but of the things you may be able to remember, I would suggest that most of them never happened.

Moses would not let the Israelites forget that God had provided for their every need. He protected them from their enemies. He provided both food and water in the wilderness. He guided them when the way was blurred. To remember the sheltering hand of God in the past is a source of strength for today and hope for tomorrow. The psalmist said, ". . . the Lord is the strength of my life; of whom shall I be afraid?" (PSALM 27:1).

Simon Peter was impetuous. He spoke and acted impulsively. He was always busy doing something, wise or foolish. His blunders, foolish words, and inconsistencies draw out our sympathy. There were times in Peter's life when he thought he knew more than the Master. In spite of his dedication to the Master, he made many mistakes. On the last night of our Lord's earthly life, Peter pledged his allegiance to Jesus. "Even if I must die with You," he declared, "I will not deny You." Fidelity could not be expressed more emphatically.

The faith Peter expressed so confidently in the upper room faded under the pressure of fear. He denied ever knowing Jesus. How could he ever forget such an ugly deed! Such a night, which was so indelibly etched in the heart of Peter, could not be forgotten.

More important, however, was the morning when Jesus ate

breakfast with Peter and some of the other disciples in the Galilean hills. Peter would never forget that morning. That was the time Christ assured him that he had a place in the Kingdom. Then the Master sent him out to feed the sheep. A broken relationship had been restored; Peter had been forgiven.

Peter became a pillar in the early church. He preached in spite of the fact that his faith might have cost him his life. Many people were converted under his ministry, and legend reports that Peter suffered martyrdom in Rome at the time of the persecutions by Nero. Tradition tells us that, during the height of the persecutions, Peter's friends prevailed upon him to flee for his life. On the way out of the city, Peter saw a vision of his Master going toward Rome. He fell down before Jesus and asked, "Where are You going, Master?" Jesus replied, "To Rome, to be crucified anew." Peter turned back and walked to the city, where he was arrested and condemned to be crucified. He requested that he be crucified with his head down, because he did not feel worthy to be crucified as his Lord had been. He could not forget the past, and the presence of the Master kept him from being afraid.

If we want to face the future with confidence, we should take a quick look at the past. We have faced many disappointments and hardships. There have been sorrows through which most of us have passed. Days have been dreary and nights have been lonely. Most of us have come to the place where we wanted to give up and quit. All those experiences are in the past. We have managed, with God's help, to overcome them. We have shouldered loads we feared would crush us. We have mastered problems we thought would defeat us, and conquered mountains we did not believe we could climb. When we look at the past, we recognize that God has been with us, and the words of the psalmist take on fresh meaning: "Thou hast beset me behind and before, and laid thine hand upon me" (PSALM 139:5).

If we want to face tomorrow with confidence, we must do our best today. The man who refuses to give his best efforts to the tasks of today will not be prepared to meet the demands of tomorrow. When we do the tasks of each day well, we may be certain that tomorrow will not ask of us a task we are not prepared to perform.

That advice may be trite, but it is still true. No man can give his best to the duties at hand if he divides his attention between the problems of yesterday, the hopes of tomorrow, and the duties of today. I am saying what others have been saying for generations, and that is: live one day at a time.

Recently I was talking to a doctor in a hospital corridor outside a patient's room. He told me what he had prescribed for the patient. "It's an old drug," he remarked, "but it works, and that is all I am interested in right now." My advice may be an old prescription, but it works, and that's all I am interested in right now. I do know that unless we are faithful to the work of today, we will not be ready to face tomorrow. No student can understand the principles of calculus without first having some understanding of algebra and geometry. Unless we learn the lessons life teaches today, we cannot hope to face the future victoriously.

The campus of Northwestern University in Evanston, Illinois, is on the shore of Lake Michigan. There is a bronze plaque on that campus in honor of Edward W. Spencer. Over a hundred years ago there was a boat wreck on Lake Michigan, and Edward W. Spencer was on the scene. He heard the screams of frightened and dying men and women, and swam out into the swirling waters sixteen times and saved seventeen persons from death. Finally, he fell to the ground, exhausted. While gasping for breath, he was heard to say, "Did I do my best? Did I do my best?"

None of us would deny the fact that Edward W. Spencer did his best. What answer would we give to that same question when asked in relation to our lives? Have we done our best? Let us consider this question in the light of all our relationships with other people.

Finally, if we are able to face tomorrow without being afraid, we must learn to trust God. I was talking to a young man who has a brilliant mind and could make a marvelous contribution to society. "I can't believe in God," he said, "because I have never seen God." "Do you believe in love?" I asked him. "Yes," he replied. "Have you ever seen love?" I responded. "That's different," he continued, "Love is a relationship and a feeling that you have toward someone else." "Well," I said, "I believe in God because of my relationship to Him, not because I have seen Him."

I went on to tell the young man that each day I talk with God and I know He is real. "Suppose," I said to him, "that someone called you from New York and talked with you on the telephone. Just suppose that you did not know the person and had never seen him. When you finished with your conversation, you would believe that the person with whom you had been talking existed." "Of course I would," he replied. "You would have a hard time convincing the many people who talk with God each day that He does not exist. They believe in Him and trust Him, not because they have seen Him, but because of the relationship they have with Him."

Some find it rather easy to trust in God as long as they live in the sunshine and on the mountain peaks of victory. When the clouds descend, the winter wind blows, and they find themselves in the shadow of misfortune, they entertain some doubts concerning God's love and care, and even His very existence. Their faith in God hinges on the circumstances of life.

It is foolish to conclude that God's love and care are measured either by the victories we know or the defeats we suffer. We test our faith, not during the days of sunshine, but when the nights are darkest.

A mighty ship proves its worthiness, not in the calm waters of a harbor where it is sheltered from the rolling waves of the ocean, but in the midst of the gigantic waves that break over its bow. So it is with our Christian faith.

We do not commit ourselves to God only during days of good health and prosperity, but for all of life. The psalmist proclaimed his unswerving faith in the adequacy of God's grace: "Yea, though I walk through the valley of the shadow of death, I will

· 151 ·

fear no evil . . ." (PSALM 23:4). The psalmist had committed his life to God, not only for the days of victory, but for the moments when the shadows would surround him.

As a minister, I am frequently called upon to unite young couples in marriage. I like the phrase "till death us do part." It is a tragedy that so many take it so frivolously. Nevertheless they promise God and each other that they will live together, even though the future may bring sickness instead of health. They pledge their love, each to the other, whether they find a pot of shining gold or the hardships of poverty down life's winding road.

Our commitment to God must be equally complete. Our faith in His love and mercy is for all of life. This is difficult for some to achieve, but unless we can reach these heights in our trust, our faith is totally inadequate.

Ella Wheeler Wilcox wrote a verse that has come to be one of my favorites. It expresses undaunted faith in the face of defeat and disappointment:

> I will not doubt, though all my ships at sea
>   Come drifting home with broken masts and sails;
>   I will believe the Hand which never fails,
>   From seeming evil worketh good for me;
> And, though I weep because those sails are battered,
>   Still will I cry, while my best hopes lie shattered,
>   "I trust in Thee."

Whatever the future holds for us, we can be sure that God stands in each tomorrow, offering the hope we need to keep trying, giving the strength we need to bear our burdens, and supplying the faith we must have in order to see how to walk when the way is blurred.

You and I will never live on the spiritual heights for which God created us unless we walk with Him, give life our best, and trust Him. There just isn't any other road that leads to victory.

18

Discovering God's Will Through Prayer

"Everybody loves somebody sometime," is a line in a popular song. We love because it is necessary to fulfill our purpose. We love because we cannot help it. I want to change this line a little and use it in connection with prayer: "Everybody prays to something sometime."

Did you ever consider the question, Why do we pray? We pray because we cannot help it. We pray because it is evident to us that we cannot reach our destiny without the help of some power beyond ourselves. We pray because the path of life leads us through dark valleys and up hills that are too much for us.

Even people who do not profess a profound faith in God, pray. Hugh Walpole's Vanessa says to Benjie, in response to Benjie's question, "Why do you love me?" "I love you because you are all that I have in the world; because without you, I am always lonely; because I am not alive without you." Before that, Vanessa and Benjie had talked about God. Benjie did not believe in God, but Vanessa did. Then Benjie took Vanessa's hand and kissed it. "God helping me," he said, "you will not regret it. Although I don't believe in Him, I expect Him to help me, you see." The need for prayer is so great, and the urge is so strong, that you will find a prayer brewing in the hearts of people everywhere.

Some people think of God as a cold computer sending back His sometimes cruel and impersonal answers to requests. Little wonder such people lose interest in prayer. We will never begin to understand prayer until we learn to think of God as a Father. In the true sense of the word, a father is one who loves his children and who has both an interest in, and a concern for, the welfare of his children.

To make certain we understand the full impact of God's love and interest in us, Jesus explained this "Father" characteristic of God and its relation to prayer: ". . . what man is there of you, whom if his son ask bread, will he give him a stone? Or if he ask a fish, will he give him a serpent? If ye then, being evil, know how to give good gifts unto your children, how much more shall your Father which is in heaven give good things to them that ask him?" (MATTHEW 7:9-11).

It may be hard for us to bring the deep hurts of the heart to some strange force in the universe which we do not understand, or to some power that is so great we cannot define it or even imagine it. Prayer is made easier when we come to believe that we are praying to a God who is like a perfect Father. When we see God as a perfect Father, we are never afraid to approach Him when the way is hard and sorrow fills our hearts.

Some people think it is futile to pray. We live in a world governed by law, they suggest. The movements of the earth and planets have been plotted for centuries yet unborn. We do not need God any more, they reason. We just have to take life as it comes. To follow this philosophy to its logical conclusion, we need not pray for the sick, nor will it do any good to pray for strength. God placed the universe in motion, and it cannot be altered. Those who feel this way fail to see the truth behind and beyond the laws which they believe have imprisoned God.

It would be inconceivable to think of life without these laws. They are for our own good, and God expects us to cooperate with them. Bring upon the scene intelligence, and these laws can be used for our advantage.

There is a law that an object heavier than air cannot fly. Yet just the other day I boarded a giant airplane that weighed over a hundred tons and flew halfway across the nation within a few hours. There is a law that the wind will push an object in the direction it blows. But a poet pointed out:

> One ship drives east and another west,
>   While the selfsame breezes blow;
> 'Tis the set of the sail and not the gale
>   That bids them where to go.

Ella Wheeler Wilcox

Water will not flow uphill, but that does not keep us from building bathrooms upstairs. You see, we have learned to manipulate natural laws and make them our servants.

There isn't anything evil about the laws that govern the universe. You plant a bulb in the fall, and it will grow and bloom in the spring. Take a high-powered automobile and drive it down the road at seventy miles an hour and ram it into a tree, and you are likely to get killed.

Natural laws do not handcuff God; rather, they are a part of God's intelligent plan for His universe. Prayer must be based on the faith that God is never baffled, never defeated, and never at His wits' end. He has a will in every set of circumstances, and if He cannot take us around the dark chasms of life, He will provide a little light by which we can walk safely through the shadows.

Aunt Jane advised Vanessa, "Don't be frightened, my dear. Trust God. . . . Life's a dangerous thing, my dear, and you can't escape the danger by staying in bed all day or making other people act for you. Don't expect things to be easy. Why should they be? God doesn't arrange the universe only for me—not for you, either . . . the way some people talk . . . you'd think that every time they have a toothache, God ought to be ashamed of Himself."

We often make requests that God refuses to answer. It is when God says "No" to a fervent request that most of us begin to doubt. We wonder if God really hears us, and if He does, why does He refuse us? God's refusals reflect His love and wisdom.

Someone gave me a shiny knife once. When my son Randall was about three years of age, he saw it and wanted to hold it. I placed the knife in his little hand and he asked me to open it for him. I had to deny his request. He could not understand, and I am certain he thought that I did not love him. My refusal to let him have an open knife was based on my love and wisdom. I knew that someday he would understand that "No" was the only answer a wise father could give.

I am sure that each person who reads these lines has been disappointed in prayer, but I am also certain that many have had prayers answered. Some are ready to give up praying when God says "No" to a request. No good mechanic would give up after a first look if he failed to find the reason why the engine of a car skipped. No physician would quit practicing his profession if he failed to find the cause of a pain in his patient. No student would give up math if he did not get the right answer. I like the words of a poet who wrote:

> I've prayed many prayers when no answer came,
>   Though I waited patient and long,
> But answers have come to enough of my prayers,
>   To make me keep praying on.

Anonymous

When life's load gets heavy, you can do one of three things:

(1) You can give up. You can conclude that there is no help and you are defeated. Six months ago, I talked to a man who had given up. The load life had placed on his shoulders seemed too much. He was headed toward a drunkard's grave. He felt no one wanted or needed him. I told him God had a place for him if he would do his part. Today he is a changed man. I saw him the other day, and that radiant look is coming back to his face.

(2) You can grit your teeth and walk on in sheer determination. You can resolve to win the battle with mere human strength. I like to see a person with courage and perseverance, but they will not take you very far down the road. You must have more.

(3) You can look up and ask God to help you. When you have exhausted your strength and done all you know how to do, you can come to God, and He will never fail you. I do not mean that He will lift from your shoulder the heavy weight you bear, but He will give you grace to bear it. I do not mean that He will take you around the valley of sorrow, but He will walk through it with you. I do not mean that He will keep you from getting hurt, but He will comfort you when you are wounded.

God does not want to disappoint us. He does not like to see His children hurt, but we cannot go through life without the scars of some hard battles. God knows that our disappointments will heal and they need not defeat us.

When I was a small lad, I asked for an electric train. That was just at the beginning of World War II, and there was a priority on steel. It was almost impossible to find an electric train. But I got the train that Christmas, and that was more than twenty-five years ago.

I didn't know until recently the demands I was placing on my father when I asked for the train. My father made less than twenty dollars a week, and he was trying to feed and clothe his five children. But he bought me a train. Just before Christmas, a very wealthy man called and asked to buy the train. Price was no consideration. My mother and father discussed selling the train. They could take the money and buy something else for me, and still have money left. It would take them a long time, paying a dollar a week, to pay for the train. They decided to keep the train and give it to me for Christmas. They didn't want to disappoint me. I still have that train. I prize it highly. It is mine because of a great sacrifice my parents made.

A long time ago God made a sacrifice for all of us. It cost Him more than we can imagine. He didn't want us to be disappointed in life, and He sent His Son to the cross in order to redeem us.

Roy M. Pearson wrote, "Prayer is not a lazy substitute for work. It is not a short cut to skill or knowledge. And, sometimes, God delays the answer to our prayer in final form, until we have time to build up the strength, accumulate the knowledge, or fashion the character that would make it possible for Him to say 'yes' to what we ask." We should think of prayer as a channel to discover God's will and never an aid to get what we want. It is human to pray for easy loads, but let us never forget to pray for strong backs. Some may pray to be excused from the battlefields, but let us always pray for the fortitude to stand as faithful soldiers as we face the inevitable battles of life. Madam Chiang Kai-shek once said, "I used to pray that God would do this or that. Now I pray that God will make His Will known to me."

When we commit our thoughts and wishes to God in prayer, we must learn to trust Him. James Hervey expressed it this way:

> Good when He gives, supremely good,
> Nor less when He denies,
> E'en crosses from His sovereign hand
> Are blessings in disguise.

Jesus taught us to pray, "Thy will be done." When we learn to pray with perfect trust, we can face life with perfect confidence, believing that God will give us what is best. We do not always want, or even know what is best for us.

Not long ago, little Richard had to go to the doctor. After a careful examination the doctor said, "I hate to do this, but he must have a shot of penicillin." Little Richard didn't want that shot, but because it was best for him he had to take it.

The man prays best who always prays, "Thy will be done." Prayer will be more satisfying when we think of God as a Father, and when we are willing to say, in the words of Eliza Hickok:

> I leave my prayer to Him alone
> Whose Will is wiser than my own.